BOOKS FOR THE COUNTRY, *continued.*

Price-2s. in boards.

The Rat. With Anecdotes. By UNCLE JAMES.

Wild Flowers: Where to Find and How to Know Them. Illustrated. By SPENCER THOMSON.

Haunts of the Wild Flowers. By ANNE PRATT.

Rarey on Horse Taming.

Sibson's Agricultural Chemistry.

Our Native Song Birds. By BARNESBY.

Our Farm of Four Acres.

Hardy Shrubs. By W. D. PRIOR.

How to Farm Profitably. 3rd Series. By MECHI.

Gardening at a Glance.

The Calendar of the Year. By Rev. J. G. WOOD.

THE FINE EDITION,

Printed on superior paper, in a large type, with the Plates printed in Colours, fcap. 8vo, gilt edges. Price 3s. 6d. each.

Common Objects of the Sea Shore. By Rev. J. G. WOOD.

Common Objects of the Country. By Rev. J. G. WOOD.

Our Woodlands, Heaths, and Hedges. By COLEMAN.

British Ferns and Allied Plants. By MOORE.

British Butterflies. By COLEMAN.

British Birds' Eggs and Nests. By ATKINSON.

Wild Flowers. By SPENCER THOMSON.

Common Objects of the Microscope. By Rev. J. G. WOOD.

Haunts of the Wild Flowers. By ANNE PRATT.

The Kitchen and Flower Garden.* E. S. DELAMER.

The Fresh and Salt-Water Aquarium. Rev. J. G. WOOD.

Common British Beetles. By Rev. J. G. WOOD.

Chamber and Cage Birds.* By BECHSTEIN.

The Calendar of the Months.* Rev. J. G. WOOD.

Common British Moths. Rev. J. G. WOOD.

Roses : A Handbook of How, When, and Where to Purchase, Propagate, and Plant Them. With 8 pp. Coloured Illusts. By W. D. PRIOR.

Gardening at a Glance. With many Illustrations, cr. 8vo. By GEORGE GLENNY.

Hardy Shrubs. With Illustrations and Coloured Plates, cr. 8vo. By W. D. PRIOR.

The Seaside Naturalist. By Rev. R. W. FRASER.

Our Garden Friends and Foes. With more than 200 Woodcuts and full-page Plates. Rev. J. G. WOOD.

* These have plain Woodcuts

NEW LETTER WRITER

FOR

THE USE OF GENTLEMEN

WITH APPLICATIONS FOR SITUATIONS

AND A COPIOUS

𝔄𝔭𝔭𝔢𝔫𝔡𝔦𝔵 𝔬𝔣 𝔉𝔬𝔯𝔪𝔰 𝔬𝔣 𝔄𝔡𝔡𝔯𝔢𝔰𝔰, 𝔅𝔦𝔩𝔩𝔰, 𝔕𝔢𝔠𝔢𝔦𝔭𝔱𝔰

AND OTHER USEFUL MATTER

LONDON

GEORGE ROUTLEDGE AND SONS

BROADWAY, LUDGATE HILL

NEW YORK: 9, LAFAYETTE PLACE.

Published in Great Britain in 2012 by Old House books & maps,
Midland House, West Way, Botley, Oxford OX2 0PH, United Kingdom.
44-02 23rd Street, Suite 219, Long Island City, NY 11101, USA.
Website: www.oldhousebooks.co.uk
© 2012 Old House.

Every attempt has been made by the Publishers to secure the appropriate
permissions for materials reproduced in this book. If there has been any
oversight we will be happy to rectify the situation and a written
submission should be made to the Publishers.

A CIP catalogue record for this book is available from the British Library.

ISBN-13: 978 1 90840 216 5

Originally published c. 1890 by George Routledge & Sons, London.

Printed in China through Worldprint Ltd.
12 13 14 15 16   10 9 8 7 6 5 4 3 2 1

FOREWORD

In the 120 years since this odd little book was written, we are supposed to have abandoned the civilised art of letter writing. It is true that most of us no longer spend hours each morning sitting at an ink blotter, filling up sheets of paper with requests and thank yous, and the 'I remain, Sir, your obedient servant' kind of formality has largely passed away, but those of us who work at a desk in front of a computer screen still spend between a third and a half of our day writing 'letters'. We just happen to call them email.

The charm of this book is that it reminds us how little has really changed. We may not share the same pressing need for advice about going into Holy Orders or tips on how to frame an informative letter from an Australian gold mine ('it is a rough life and some of the characters you meet with require a little caution') but we still fall in love, we still want to 'get on in life', we still are late paying bills ('I am sorry to be unable to pay you the balance of your account, but will do my utmost to send it at the end of this week, or the beginning of next, without fail') and we still need and like to complain.

As so often with self-help books (or 'self-improvement' to use the proper Victorian term) the useful advice becomes overwhelmed by the distracting detail. For every fawning, circumlocutory letter requesting help or expressing thanks – and if anyone wants a masterclass in high Victorian simpering, look no further – there are others where the characters in the story take over. I particularly like the one from a farmer to his son:

> Our old horse, Dobbs, died yesterday. He has been for a long time fit for but little, but he was so old a favourite that I could

> not find it in my heart to have him shot. The other live stock, including your favourite pigeons are doing well, but we have missed several chickens of late...

Suddenly we seem to have strayed into the middle of a story. We've forgotten this is supposed to be a practical guide: we want to know more about poor Dobbs and solve the mystery of the missing chickens.

Then there are the letters of which the editors disapprove:

> When you remember where you sat last night at the playhouse, you will not need to be told that this comes from the person who was just before you.

It turns out the young man has a shop in Henrietta Street and 'has been but two years in trade' but it still feels a bit too close to stalking and the editors leave us in no doubt, adding a note: 'The above is a specimen of a style of letter too frequently sent, but we hope few of our readers will think of writing on such a subject, with no better title to acquaintance.'

Quite so – which makes it baffling that they decided to include it, or the passionate love letters, which they disown 'on the grounds of plain common sense... but people *will* send such letters!' It's as though they couldn't quite deny themselves a bit of vicarious excitement.

It is these contradictions and divagations that make this book a small classic of its kind. It may not be of much practical use to us emailers and texters, but it bristles with recognisable detail. Reading it is like strolling across a host of unwritten Victorian novels, picking up traces of snobbery and dashed expectations, money troubles and stifled passions. The past may be another country, but we can still speak the language.

John Mitchinson, 2012
Director of Research for QI and co-author of
The QI Book of General Ignorance

TABLE OF CONTENTS,

Arranged under the respective subjects of which the Letters hereafter treat.

ACCOUNTS, proposals to open, *Letter* 40, 156.
    Ditto, with publishers, 41.
Advice and assistance applied for, 23.
Apprentice, proposing son as, 126.
Assistance sought on behalf of another, 31.
———— from an old friend by one in adverse circumstances, 37.
———— answers to ditto, 38, 39.
Bill, delaying payment of, 87. [*See* DEBTS.]
Book, loan of asked, 32.
——— answers to request of, 33, 34.
——— returning ditto, 35.
——— asking subscriptions to, 81, 82; answers to, 83; for return of ditto to a library, 147.
Brother, to a sister abroad, 75; to a sister in London, 76.
Building (or other) Society, application for shares in a, 67.
Clergyman, letter about rent, 133; on being elected churchwarden 134.
Clerkship, application for, 27.
———— testimonial on behalf of applicant for, 28.
———— answer to communication from firm respecting, 29.
College, letter from a merchant to the master of a, 1.
——— answer from president of to ditto, 2.
——— from a young man at Oxford to his father, 2.
Colonies, letters from, 80.
Daughter, letter to about her suitor, 120.
Debts, applications for, 47 48, 49, 51, 57.

CONTENTS.

Debts, answers to, and excuses of not meeting ditto, 50, 52, 53, **54, 55,** 58, 87, 90, 93, 151, 152.

Education, complaint of neglected, 17. [*See* SCHOOL.]

Footman, answer to advertisement for, 26.

Gardener, application for situation as, 25.

Gold diggings, letter from, 77, 78; to sweetheart in London, **79.**

Holy Orders, advice respecting, 148, 149.

Horse-dealer, letter to, 145, answer, 146.

House-agent, letter to about letting, 45.

Invitations, to a bachelor party, 69; to dinner, 70; to a water-party, **71;** to a pic-nic, 72, 73, 74.

Loan, application for, 59, 61; ditto on insurance, 66.

—— answers to ditto, 60, 62, 63, 64, 65.

London, to a friend in, with a commission, 44, 141; **answer to ditto,** 142; about badness of goods, 143; answer, 144.

Matrimonial, after meeting at a party, 94; on longer acquaintance, **95;** on receiving a favourable answer, 96; to a widow, 97; to father of lady, 98, 113; answers to ditto, 99, 100, 114, 115; to one to whom one is engaged, 101; to ditto, complaining of not receiving a letter, 102; to ditto, on her birthday, 103; on a misunderstanding, 103, 104, 117; warning against a doubtful match, 105; letters from young tradesmen, 106, 108, 110; to an early playmate, 107; in reference to confessing an attachment, 108, 109; various proposals, 111, 112; **pro-posing day for nuptials, 116;** discontinuing addresses, 118; **from a** man-servant to a maid-servant, 119; from a soldier, **122.**

Money, acknowledging, 56. [*See* DEBTS, &c.]

—— in letters, enclosing, 153, **154, 155.**

Note of hand, renewal of, 90.

Notes and Cards, page 90.

Organist, application as, 140.

Parish doctor, application for, 138; ditto clerk, **139.**

Partnership, recommendation to, 125.

Physician, letter to, for advice, 124.

Public school, application respecting, 22.

Railway, application for situation on, 24, **46.**

Recommending a successor, 125; to a relieving officer for assistance, **135.**

Rent, delaying payment of, 91, 92, 134.

Schoolmaster, letter to, about son, 4.

—————— Parish, application for situation as, 30

CONTENTS.

School, letter to son at, 5.
—— from boy at, to father, 6.
—————————— to both parents, 7.
—— ditto about the vacation, 8.
—— for a present, 9.
—— to a daughter at, from a widower, 10.
—— to a son or daughter at, 18.
—— from an officer to a son at, 19.
—— answer to the same, 20.
—— letter respecting improvement of son at, 21.
——application for interest towards introducing a child into a public, 22; into a public free school, 88.
Servant in place, letter to, 127; from her sweetheart, 128.
Shares, application for, 67; transferring ditto, 68.
Situation, application for, 36.
Son, letter to on his marriage, 121; from a labourer, 129; from a farm-house, 130.
Soldier, to his parents, 123; to his sweetheart, 122.
Subscriptions asked, to books, 81, 82; to charities, 84; on behalf of the sick, 89; answers to ditto, 83, 85, 86.
Theatrical manager, 137.
Tutor, letter seeking recommendation of one, 11.
—— ditto, recommending one, 12.
—— ditto, from gentlemen to tutor, 13.
—— reply of tutor, 14.
—— from tutor to former pupil at college, 15.
—— letter to from pupil, 16.
Veterinary surgeon, letter to, 131; answer from, 182.
Water Company, letter to, 136
Widow. [See MATRIMONIAL.]

APPENDIX.

Wills— Various forms, 100 to 106.
Bonds   „   „   106—107.
Public Company—Transfer of share, 107.
   „   „   Form of proxy, 108.
Petitions and Memorials, 109.
Receipts, Bills, &c.—Forms, 111.

—◆◆—

THE LADIES' AND GENTLEMEN'S LETTER
WRITER, 1*s*.

THE COMMERCIAL LETTER WRITER, 1*s*.

THE LADIES' LETTER WRITER, 6*d*.

THE GENTLEMEN'S LETTER WRITER, 6*d*.

THE LOVERS' LETTER WRITER, 6*d*.

THE CHILD'S LETTER WRITER, 6*d*.

THE

GENTLEMAN'S LETTER-WRITER.

LETTER I.

From a Merchant in London, to the Master of a College, recommending his Son to his care as a pupil.

London, January 17th, 18—.

REV. SIR,—The high opinion I have long entertained of your character as a scholar and a gentleman, encourages me to solicit your kind assistance in an affair of very great importance.

My son Charles has just completed his course of studies at Merchant Taylors' School, and is desirous of being entered as a commoner in your College. The variety of business in which I am engaged requires my constant residence in London; but, being anxious to procure for my dear boy every advantage within my power, I feel that there is no gentleman in Oxford, to whose fidelity I could so readily trust him as to yourself. Should you, therefore, feel disposed to honour my son by admitting him as a member of your college, you will confer a great favour upon,

Sir,

Your most obedient servant,

To the Rev ——.

(——).

LETTER II.
The Answer.

St. Chad's, Bullford, Jan. 19th, 18--.

DEAR SIR,—Although —— College is very full just now, and we generally expect a longer notice from candidates for matriculation; still, both from my personal respect for yourself, and my desire to advance any young man who has already acquitted himself in so creditable a manner as your son appears to have done, I will do my best to accommodate him with rooms. It will be necessary for him to be at —— on the —— instant. A moderate knowledge of Homer and Virgil, and of Latin composition, will be all that is required for the matriculation examination, and I doubt not that he will be fully up to our standard.

I remain, dear Sir, your very faithful servant,

To ——, Esq.   (————).

LETTER III.
From a Young Man who has recently entered College.

St. Chad's, Bullford, April 17th, 18—.

MY DEAR FATHER,—I am happy to inform you that I passed my preliminary examination with tolerable credit, and that Dr. —— was kind enough to compliment me on my Latin style. My former schoolmate —— has paid me much attention, and, as he moves in the best set in College, I am in hopes of establishing a pleasant and profitable acquaintance, without running into extravagance, or defeating the whole purpose of my collegiate career. I need hardly tell you, my dear father, that University society is of a most mixed character; and it is not easy to ascertain at once whom it is advisable to know. At the same time, I trust to avoid the superciliousness which seems to be affected by many men down here, and to enjoy the many healthy recreations for which we have so many facilities, without giving either you or myself any cause for regretting the day that first saw me an University man.

Present my kindest love to my dear mother and sisters, and assure them that even a college life does not prevent my feeling a strong yearning after home. But I shall look forward to seeing all of you at our ensuing grand commemoration, when Bullford will be swarming with visitors

The cheque you so kindly sent me arrived in due course, and was not only fully adequate to the expenses of my entrance, but has left a surplus which will last me throughout the term

Believe me, my dear Father,

Your affectionate Son,

To ——, Esq.

(———).

LETTER IV.

To a Schoolmaster.

Doncaster, 15th April, 18—.

SIR,—I regret that the pressure of business prevents my accompanying my son down to —— House, as I should gladly have had a few minutes' conversation with you, relative to his future course of studies. At the same time, I have such thorough confidence both in your will and capability to train youth in a manner calculated to render them useful to themselves and others, that I unhesitatingly entrust my dear boy to your charge, only hoping that he may prove worthy of the attention which I feel persuaded he will receive at your hands.

I have the honour to remain, Sir,

Your very obedient and faithful servant,

To ——.

(———).

LETTER V.

To a Son at school.

Doncaster, 17th Oct. 18—.

MY DEAR SON,—I am delighted to hear of your progress, and send you a little remittance of pocket-money, to prove to you that I am ever ready to give encouragement where it is deserved. You must always bear in mind that upon your career at school much of your future life must depend. To waste the precious hours of youth is to make preparation for a useless and dishonourable old age; whereas by steady industry, care of that health with which God has happily blessed you, and submission to those who have the best right, as well as the best inclination, to advise you for your good, you may hope to ripen into a respectable and useful member of society, and to render yourself fit to encounter those responsibilities which

fall to every man's lot. Your mother unites in hearty wishes
that you may go on as you have begun, and that your whole
life may prove a credit to yourself, and a comfort to us. Make
our best respects to your excellent preceptor, and believe me,

Your affectionate Father,

To Master ——.   (———).

LETTER VI.

From a Boy at school to his Father

Huddersfield, July 20th, 18—.

MY DEAR FATHER,—Many thanks for your kind present and
valuable advice. I sincerely hope that your good opinion of
me will long remain unchanged, and that I may be able to do
justice to the strenuous exertions and kindly attention of my
excellent preceptor.

I am at present working very hard, and hope to gain one
step higher in the school before the end of the quarter. My
schoolfellows are, generally speaking, very agreeable and well-
disposed boys, and we are so well treated, that I feel almost as
happy as if I were at home. Nevertheless, I often think of
the coming vacation with not a little eagerness, and long to
meet you and my dear mother, brothers, and sisters, and to
enjoy the Christmas festivities in the way we have always been
accustomed.

I remain, my dear Father,
Your affectionate and grateful son,

To ——, Esq.   (———).

LETTER VII.

From the same to both Parents.

Huddersfield, July 30th, 18—.

MY DEAR PARENTS,—It will, doubtless, give you much pleasure to learn that, owing to the unremitting attention of the
Rev. Mr. ——, I have made so satisfactory a progress, that I
have not only been removed one class higher in the school, but
have carried off the second prize for Latin verse.

I sincerely hope that I may continue sufficiently industrious to keep up to all the expectations you have formed of me, and which you have spared no pains or expense to realise. With mingled feelings of regret at leaving my kind preceptor, and of delight at the prospect of our speedy meeting for the holidays,

I remain, my dearest parents,

With kindest love to all at home,

Your affectionate and dutiful Son,

To Mr. and Mrs. ——.　　　　　　　　　　　(————).

LETTER VIII.

From the same, announcing the coming Vacation.

Holloway, Nov. 15th, 18—.

DEAR (FATHER *or* MOTHER),—It is with mingled feelings of regret and pleasure that I announce to you the conclusion of one half year's stay at school. On the 24th inst. I shall hope to return home, and, if I may judge by the opinion Dr. —— has expressed of my conduct, I trust you will not be dissatisfied with my progress during the last five months.

I remain, dear ——

Your affectionate and dutiful son,

To ——.　　　　　　　　　　　　　　(————).

LETTER IX.

Returning thanks for a Present.

DEAR MAMMA,—I was no less delighted with your kind letter than with the present it accompanied. Knowing, as I do, that your whole life is occupied in promoting my improvement and happiness, I can only feel that each fresh token of your affection lays an additional claim upon my gratitude.

Dr. and Mrs. —— unite in their best compliments and wishes for your health, for which, believe me, I pray night and day.

Your affectionate and grateful son,

To ——　　　　　　　　　　　　　　(———-).

LETTER X.

A Widower to his Daughter at school.

London, June 14 th, 18—.

MY DEAR,—Your last letter gave me much pleasure, as it conveyed to me the belief that, although enjoying every comfort under the care of Miss ——, you still cling with fondness to your home and to your father.   Believe me, my dearest child, it was no small trial for me to part with you after my unhappy bereavement, but I felt that parental fondness must not be instrumental to making a sacrifice of a child's prospects, and that nothing can excuse a man debarring his children of the necessary advantages of education, in order to gratify the somewhat pardonable desire to see them around his own fireside. I trust, my dear girl, that when you return to —— your improvement in all that can elevate the character of a young woman will be ample atonement for the sorrow I feel in your temporary estrangement from me.   Pray write me another letter soon, and believe me,

Your ever affectionate father,

To Miss ——.   (———)

LETTER XI.

From a Gentleman seeking a recommendation to a Tutor for his Son.

Scarborough, June 4th, 18—.

MY DEAR ——,—Your large acquaintance among men of education leads me to believe that you could materially assist me in a matter which I have much at heart.   My son —— is now of age sufficient to render strict attention to his education of importance.   Wishing, however, to give him due preparation before sending him to a public school, I write to ask w ether you are acquainted with any gentleman who would be willing to undertake the office of private tutor for the next two or three years.

As I am convinced of the importance of laying a good foundation, before we attempt to elevate the superstructure of education, I should gladly offer a liberal remuneration to any gentleman on whose fitness for the office I could thoroughly depend.

I trust the importance of the matter will be my best excuse for troubling you with it, and remain,

> My dear ——,
>
> Yours ever faithfully,

To ——, Esq. (————).

———

LETTER XII.

The Answer.

> Chester, June 6th, 18—.

MY DEAR ——,—I lose no time in replying to your letter, as I not only feel complimented by your reliance on my judgment, but am fortunately acquainted with a gentleman who is every way likely to suit your views. Mr. —— is a very old acquaintance of mine, and has not only taken high classical honours himself, but has been almost uniformly successful with his pupils. Being at present partially disengaged, he would be willing to devote a few hours every day to the instruction of your son; and, from all I know of his character and attainments, I feel certain that you will have no cause to regret selecting him to an office of such vital importance to your son's future welfare.

I enclose Mr. ——'s present address, and, in the sincere hope that your correspondence may prove satisfactory to both parties,

> I remain, my dear ——,
>
> Yours ever truly,

To ——, Esq. (————).

———

LETTER XIII.

From a Gentleman to a Tutor.

> London, July 4th, 18—.

SIR,—My friend Mr. —— has spoken in such high terms of your capabilities as a private tutor, that I am anxious to know

whether your present engagements will admit of your undertaking the preparation of my son for school (*or* college, *as the
case may be*) during the next year or two.   He is just — years
of age, and, as far as I may be allowed to judge, possesses fair
abilities and much amiability of character.   An early communication from you, relative to time, remuneration, and other
matters, will greatly oblige,

Sir,

Your obedient servant,

To the Rev. ——.   (————).

LETTER XIV

The Answer.

London, July 6th, 18—.

Sir,—I feel much flattered at Mr. ——'s favourable mention
of myself, and shall be most happy to devote two hours a day
to the instruction of your son (*state the time for the lessons*).
Having devoted so much of my life to educational occupations,
I venture to express a hope that no care or exertion will be
wanting on my part to satisfy your most earnest wishes for
your son's welfare.

My usual terms are (*state them*), which I presume will be
satisfactory.

I remain, Sir,

Your very obedient servant,

To ——, Esq.   (————).

LETTER XV.

From a Tutor to a former Pupil, now at College.

Shrewsbury, Jan. 29th, 18—.

My dear ——,—I sincerely hope this brief epistle from an
old friend and preceptor will not be thought impertinent.   I
have known you so long, that I feel assured you will receive a
few words of counsel from an older head, and that you will
believe that whatever my advice be really worth, it is at least
dictated in a kindly and a straightforward spirit.

You have entered on a style of life in which the advantages and the temptations follow each other so closely, that it is often difficult to separate the one from the other. Even the talents which procured you your scholarship may become a means of mischief if you do not exert severe control over their application and direction. But I know too much of your innate goodness of heart to believe that you will ever allow yourself to be spoilt even by success, and have a happy confidence in your integrity of character, which leads me to think you incapable of anything mean or flippant.

But, above all, my dear ——, let me exhort you never to forget the duty you owe to the God who has bestowed a share of his gifts upon you. We are all of us too apt, amidst the bustle and enterprise of every-day life, to forget Him upon whom our very life utterly depends, and to think only of worldly success, while we lose all thought of the life for which our present existence should be but a preparation. Let me express a hope, my dear ——, that you will think goodness preferable to greatness; that you will study the cultivation of the soul as well as of the mere intellect; that you will recollect how great a virtue is reliance on God, and how noble a self-reliance is the result of such virtue.

That every honourable success, and every consequent happiness may be the result of your efforts, is the sincere prayer of

Your old tutor and ever sincere friend,

To ——, Esq.   (——).

LETTER XVI.

The Answer.

Oxford, April 4th, 18—

MY DEAR SIR,—It is, indeed, delightful to receive such a letter from so valued and tried a friend. I sincerely hope that your example, as well as your conversation, has possessed sufficient influence over my conduct here to enable me to withstand some of the temptations of the place, and to think of duties higher than those which merely result from our ambition or self-satisfaction. I am happy in enjoying the society of

young men who have greater belief in conscience than in mere
talent; and I trust that, without advocating extreme views of
any kind, I am living as you would wish me, and have taught
me, to live.

My studies are progressing most satisfactorily, if, at least, I
can take success as a warrant of merit. At collections * last
time I was placed in the first class, and I have every reason to
hope for a like position this term. I have likewise gained an
exhibition, which, though small, is a useful addition to my
funds, and moreover associates me still more with the foundation † of my college. Dr. ——, the head of our college, has
paid me much kind attention; and my tutor spares no pains,
so that I have altogether much to be thankful for.

I look forward with delight to the time when we shall again
meet. Meanwhile, believe that no success can ever efface the
remembrance of the kind friend and preceptor to whom I owe
all. With sincerest wishes for your health, happiness, and
long continuance in your exemplary career of usefulness,

Believe me, my dear Sir,
Your ever affectionate pupil and friend,

To the Rev. ——.   (————).

LETTER XVII.

From a Young Man of neglected education to an old Friend.

Dulwich, 4th February, 18—.

SIR,—Since my appointment to the office of clerk in Messrs.
——'s establishment, through your kind interest, I have felt very
anxious as to my present imperfect education. Circumstances,
with which you are well acquainted, rendered my early means
of instruction very limited, and I now feel that it is high time
to remedy my deficiencies. Enjoying, as I now do, an income
sufficient to support me in respectability, I still feel unhappy in

---

* A terminal examination within college, at which the men are in
some colleges classed.
† Members are said to be on the "foundation," when they hold fel-
lowships, scholarships, or other offices for which the founder of the
college has made provision.

the consciousness of my deficiency of that general knowledge which renders a man fit for the society around him. May I solicit your advice as to the best course of reading and instruction likely to remedy this evil? I feel not only the desire, but the will, to learn, and humbly trust that, with your long experience of the world, and your knowledge of what is, in these times, required of every man, I may derive no small benefit from your advice.

Hoping that you will excuse my troubling one to whom I am already so much indebted, believe me,

Sir,

Your obliged and faithful servant,

To ——, Esq.   (———).

LETTER XVIII.

From a Gentleman to his Son, or Daughter, at school.

London, July 7th, 18—.

MY DEAR ——,—Though I have so long been silent, you have not been absent from my remembrance, and I should have written to you before, had I not waited for some intelligence which would have rendered my letter more acceptable. Nothing, however, of any particular importance has transpired, and I have, therefore, only to inform you that your mother, myself, and your brothers and sisters remain as well as when I last wrote. My knowledge of your usual good behaviour and attention to your duties, renders any fresh advice in regard to your conduct unnecessary. I leave you, my dear child, to the guidance of your own good sense, and the guardian care of (Mr. or Mrs. ——), to whom myself and your mother desire to be remembered, with our compliments to ——. Believe me, with the best wishes of myself and your dear mother for your health and happiness,

Your ever affectionate father,

To ——.   (———).

LETTER XIX.

From a Gentleman, an Officer in the army, to his Son at a boarding-school, recommending diligence in his studies.

Portsmouth, Jan. 1, 18—.

DEAR ——,—Our regiment is now at Portsmouth, and we are ordered to embark for Canada. I hoped to have called on you at school, but so sudden were our orders to march that I had no time to spare from the necessary duties of my station. Let me hope, my dear son, that you will attend to your studies with the utmost assiduity

Youth is the proper time for acquiring that knowledge, which, if properly improved and reduced to practice, will be of the utmost service to you throughout your future life. You are as yet unacquainted with the world, and happy will it be for you if you remain ignorant of the toils and dangers of a military life. Let me, therefore, entreat you, in the most earnest manner, to strive to qualify yourself for some employment which will procure you a decent subsistence, and enable you to live independently in the world. I have left an order with our agent to meet the expenses necessary for your education; and although my income is but small, yet, believe me, nothing on my part shall be wanting to make your life as comfortable as possible. As it will be some days before we sail, I shall hope to have a letter from you, and if too late, it will be sent after me. In the meantime,

I am your affectionate father,

To ——.   (——).

LETTER XX.
The Answer.

London, Jan. 3rd, 18—.

HONOURED SIR,—One of the first lessons you taught me was, that gratitude is the noblest principle that can actuate the heart of man; but what must it be, when connected with the duty incumbent on a son to so indulgent a parent! I am left in a situation that may be felt, but not described. That my dear and honoured parent should be so suddenly hurried away to a stant country almost fills me with horror, especially

when I consider, that I may never have an opportunity of seeing you any more. I am convinced that your friendly advice
to me is such that, if followed strictly, it must be attended
with the most beneficial consequences to myself: my honour
and happiness will equally depend on adhering to it, and I
shall always consider it as my second greatest duty, to obey
the precepts of my worthy father. I have gone already so far
as to be able to read ——, and next week I enter upon——. I
have some thoughts, if agreeable to you, of taking chambers in
one of the inns of court, in order to study the law: my inclinations have always run that way, but I submit it wholly to
your approbation. Let me beg to hear from you as often as
possible, as it will be the greatest pleasure I can enjoy during
such a separation.

I am,

Honoured Sir,

Your affectionate son,

To ——.   (———)

LETTER XXI

*From a Gentleman desirous of ascertaining the state of his
Son's improvement at school.*

Chelsea, October 7th, 18—.

Rev. and Dear Sir,—I write a few lines to express my
hope that the improvement of my son is such as to satisfy
both your undoubted skill and attention, and my own anxiety.
Feeling that his delicate health in early life has placed him
at some disadvantage, I am the more desirous to ascertain the
present state of his progress in your establishment.

With kindest compliments to Mrs. ——, and sincere hopes
that we may both find George all that we could wish, believe
me to remain,

Reverend and dear Sir,

Your sincerely faithful servant,

To the Rev ——   (———)

LETTER XXII.

Gentleman, soliciting his interest and assistance in intro ducing a Child into one of the public schools.

Tottenham Court Road, June 4th, 18—.

Sir,— Mr. ——, of —— street, with whom I believe you are acquainted, has kindly permitted me to make use of his name in venturing to your notice. I beg most respectfully to state that my object in writing is to solicit the favour of your kind assistance in placing one of my children, (of whom I have —— dependent on my exertions for support,) in the —— school. The son, on whose behalf I now plead, will be —— years of age on the —— of next ——: and should I, by your kind assistance, be so fortunate as to succeed in procuring him admission into that charity, I shall ever most gratefully remember your kindness.

I remain, respected Sir,
Your humble obedient servant,

To ——, Esq.   (————).

LETTER XXIII.

From a Young Man to an elderly Relative, soliciting his advice and assistance.

London, March 8th, 18—.

My dear Uncle,—From the kind manner in which you have always encouraged me to appeal to you whenever I required good advice, I am now induced to write to you. I have, as you are aware, been left to my own guidance rather more than —— years, during which period I have saved a little money. You will, I feel, do me the justice to believe me, when I state that I have avoided every kind of extravagance or indulgence that would any way have interfered with my future prospects in life, and I have, therefore, less hesitation in coming to the more immediate object of my letter. A prospect has just opened which gives me hopes that I may, by industry and perseverance, at least realise a certain and comfortable living. Mr —— of ——, who has for many years successfully carried on the business of a ——, is about to retire ; and I find that if he could obtain a suitable offer, he would be inclined to dispose of the whole concern on most favourable terms. I have, at my command, —— pounds, but the sum which Mr. —— would accept for the business is very nearly twice that amount; he is willing, however, to take security for the remainder, payable with interest in —— years. Under these circumstances, dear uncle, I appeal to you ; let me have your candid advice whether you view the offer in the same favourable light that I do, and if so, might I solicit you to become security for that part of the money which is beyond my present means of raising? I have no doubt of being able to repay it myself within the prescribed time. Your early answer will be esteemed a particular favour by

Dear uncle,

Your affectionate nephew.

To ——, Esq.   (——).

LETTER XXIV.

From a Working Man to the Secretary, or a Director, of a Railway Company.

Church Street, Shoreditch,
May 4th, 18—.

HONOURED Sir,—Feeling desirous of obtaining a situation as a —— in the service of —— railway company, for which I believe myself fully competent, having been for several years engaged as —— in the service of ——, I refer you to the enclosed letter of recommendation from Mr. ——, of ——, and Mr. ——, of ——, in my favour, which I hope may prove satisfactory. Should I, by your kind assistance, obtain the situa-

tion I seek, I will endeavour to show my sense of the obligation by a zealous and diligent discharge of my duties.

> I remain, honoured Sir,
>   Your obedient humble servant,

To ——. Esq.   (———).

LETTER XXV.

To solicit a place as Gardener.

> Battersea, 15th April, 18—.

SIR,—Understanding that there is a vacancy in your establishment for a (head *or* under) gardener, I beg to offer myself
to your notice. I have had constant experience both in
nursery-grounds and gentlemen's private gardens, and am
thoroughly acquainted with the management of the green-
house and hothouse.

I inclose some testimonials from gentlemen with whom I
have lived, which I hope will prove satisfactory. The last
situation I filled was with Mr. ——, who will, I believe, speak
favourably to my character and fitness for the office. I am a
married (*or* single) man with (*state whether any family*), and
my age is ——. Should you feel disposed to entertain my
application, a letter directed to —— will meet with prompt
attention from

> Sir,
>   Your most obedient servant,

To ——, Esq.   (———).

LETTER XXVI.

Answer to an Advertisement.

> Peter Street, Hoxton, June 4th, 18—.

SIR,—In answer to an advertisement in the *Times* of yesterday, I beg to offer myself for the situation of footman in your
family. I have lived for nearly eleven years in the family of
——, until the death of my respected employer led to my

dismissal. I trust that the inclosed testimonials will satisfy you as to my character and fitness for the duty.

I remain, Sir,

Your obedient humble servant,

To ——, Esq.   (————).

LETTER XXVII.

To a Firm, seeking a Clerkship.

Cecil Street, Strand, April 4th, 18—.

GENTLEMEN,—Perceiving by your advertisement in the —— of ——, that you are in want of a clerk, I beg to inclose testimonials, and venture to hope that from my previous experience in the line of business you pursue, I should be of some use in your establishment. My habits of life are such as to insure regularity in the discharge of my duties, and I can only assure you that, should you honour me with your confidence, I shall spare no pains to acquit myself to your satisfaction.

I remain, Gentlemen,

Your obedient servant,

To Messrs. ——.   (————).

LETTER XXVIII.

A Testimonial on behalf of a similar applicant.

Hornsey, April, 3rd, 18—.

GENTLEMEN,—Finding that Mr. —— is an applicant for a situation as clerk, I beg to say a few words on his behalf. During the —— years he was in my employ, I found him diligent and conscientious in the discharge of his duties, remarkably clever in correspondence, and correct in the management of my books. Indeed, nothing but my retiring from business would have induced me to part with him, and I firmly believe that both his personal character, and his thorough knowledge of business will render him a valuable acquisition to your firm.

I remain, Gentlemen,
Yours most obediently,

To Messrs. ——   (———).

LETTER XXIX.

A second Answer to a communication from a Firm.

Cecil Street, Strand, April 5th, 18—.

GENTLEMEN,—In answer to your question as to the salary I should expect, I beg to express my perfect satisfaction with the offer you propose, and can assure you that, should we ultimately come to terms, no pains will be spared on my part to do justice to the confidence reposed in me. With regard to the guarantee required, Mr. ——'s name will, I trust, be satisfactory.

I remain, Gentlemen,
Your obedient servant,

To Messr. ——.   (———).

LETTER XXX.

Application for a situation as Parish Schoolmaster.

London, June 30th, 18—.

GENTLEMEN,—Understanding that a vacancy for the situation of master to your parochial school has occurred, I beg to offer myself as a candidate for the situation. From the inclosed testimonials you will perceive that I officiated for some time as temporary master in —— school, and that my system both of instruction and discipline gave considerable satisfaction. Added to this, I have spent —— years at the —— training school, and am considered to be well grounded in all the knowledge required for the successful training of boys of the class for whom you wish to provide education. Should you honour me with your confidence, I trust that, by blending kindness with strict regularity and firmness of discipline, I shall give you no cause to regret your choice. I have the honour to be,

Gentlemen,

Your most obedient and humble servant,

(———).

To the Gentlemen of the Committee of the
— National School.

LETTER XXXI.

Application on behalf of another Person.

Dulwich, Oct. 1st, 18—.

MY DEAR ——,—I am at all times adverse to troubling my friends on my own behalf, but there are occasions on which I venture to trespass upon their kindness when other people are concerned. A young friend of mine, the son of a tradesman of small means, has evinced so much taste for the arts, that I venture to hope you will give him some encouragement. He has already met with some success, but is most anxious to obtain the means of completing his studies in France and Italy. Knowing your liberality in aiding the efforts of the young and deserving, I venture to hope that you will join me in contributing to a fund that is forming to aid him in his praiseworthy design, as, from what he has already produced, I feel assured he will give his friends every reason to be satisfied with the results of their kindness.

Believe me,

My dear ——,

Yours most faithfully,

To ——, Esq. (———).

LETTER XXXII.

From a Gentleman to his Friend, requesting the Loan of a Book.

London, September 7th, 18—.

SIR,—While last at your house, you showed me a book entitled ——, which I remember as a work of so much interest

that I feel much inclined to peruse it, and should esteem it a
great favour if you would lend it to me. I will take great
care of it, and return it in a few days, as I have, at present,
abundant leisure for reading.

I am, Sir,

Your obedient servant,

To ——, Esq.   (————).

LETTER XXXIII.

In Answer.

DEAR SIR,—You are quite welcome to the volume you express a wish to read; but I must ask you to let me have it by
the ——th of next month, as I shall then have occasion for it
for some literary purposes.

Believe me,

Dear Sir,

Yours very truly,

To ——, Esq.   (————).

LETTER XXXIV.

In the Negative.

MY DEAR SIR,—I have unfortunately lent the book you ask
for, but should it be returned within a reasonable time, I will
forward it to you. Regretting to be at present obliged to dis-
appoint you,

I remain,

My dear Sir,

Yours most faithfully,

To ——, Esq.   (———-)

LETTER XXXV.

A Gentleman on returning a Book he had borrowed.

London, September 16th, 18—.

DEAR SIR,—I return you the book which you were kind
enough to lend me, and, with it, accept my best thanks for

your kindness. The work is both interesting and instructive, and I have been much gratified by its perusal. If I can in any way return the favour, it will give me much pleasure to do so.

I am, Sir,
Yours, much obliged,

To ——, Esq.　　　　　　　　　　　　(——

LETTER XXXVI.

From a Young Man in the country to a Friend in town, soliciting a situation.

——, February 18th, 18—.

DEAR ——,—When you left ——, you were kind enough to promise, that should it be in your power to forward my interests in any manner, you would feel a pleasure in so doing. I am now in want of a situation, my former employer having sold his business, and his successor having, as he informs me, a sufficient number of hands for all the work he is likely to have. If, therefore, you should hear of any situation or employment which you consider likely to suit me, either in my own business, that of a ——, or in any other in which I can make myself useful, your recommendation would greatly oblige, and be of material service to,

Dear ——,
Yours very truly,

To ——, Esq.　　　　　　　　　　　　(———).

LETTER XXXVII.

From a reduced Gentleman, soliciting the aid of an old Friend.

London, 7th March, 18—.

DEAR SIR,—Though many years have elapsed since we last met, I trust that the name of —— is not entirely obliterated from your memory. It is the same ——, your former friend and intimate companion, who now addresses you; but, I lament to say, sadly changed from the individual whom you then knew. My former flow of spirits has gone long since with my prosperity, and with those who once thronged round to flatter me. Sorrow, poverty, and the sneers and contempt of an unfeeling world alone remain. This, to a man of your sensibility, must be as painful to read, as it is for me to write. It is not my object to practice on your feelings by overwrought language. But my distresses have increased to that degree, that speak they will in some guise; and, urged on by them, I have stifled my previous repugnance at disclosing them to you. Without further circumlocution, let me tell you, then, at once, that my state is that of the bitterest poverty, in fact, of destitution; and I make my appeal to your kindly feelings in the name of that friendship which once existed between us. I have said enough. I need but add my address, and subscribe myself,

Your most unfortunate friend,

To ——, Esq.   (———)

LETTER XXXVIII.

The Answer.

Canterbury, May 12th, 18—.

MY DEAR SIR,—I have just received your letter, which I know it must have cost you much pain to write, and which I must have been wanting in all friendly feeling, could I have read it unmoved. Most sincerely do I sympathize in your present sufferings, and as sincerely do I hope that some unlooked-for change of fortune may speedily relieve you from them, and eventually restore you to comfort and prosperity. As far as my good offices can extend, you may readily command them, and as some alleviation to your present necessities, I beg you will accept the inclosed (*cheque, or sum of* ——-). Should you wish to see me, and call at my house, you will meet with the reception due to an old and respected acquaintance; and with every hope that your present embarrassments may be but temporary,

Believe me,
My dear Sir,
Your ever sincere friend,

To ——, Esq.   (———).

LETTER XXXIX.

Answer, in the Negative.

Oxford, Aug. 12th, 18—.

MY DEAR SIR,—It is at all times painful to hear of the dis-tress of another, especially of one for whom one has ever felt cordial and deserved esteem—still more painful, when one's power of relieving it is so feeble as my own. The expenses of an increasing family, and the difficulties consequent upon recent losses in business, render it impossible for me to act as I unquestionably would under other circumstances. Should a more favourable change take place in my own affairs, depend upon it I will not forget so old a friend.

With every kind wish that those who have the means, as well as the will, to assist you, may speedily be forthcoming,

Believe me,

My dear Sir,

Yours most sincerely,

To ——, Esq.   (———).

LETTER XL.

To a Tradesman proposing to open an Account.

London, Feb. 7th, 18—.

SIR,—My friend, Mr. —— of B—— street, has spoken of you in terms of high recommendation; so much so, indeed, that having found reason to withdraw my orders from my late ——, I am disposed to open an account with your firm. You will therefore much oblige me by forwarding a list of prices, toge-ther with other necessary particulars as to your manner of doing business.

I am, Sir,

Your obedient servant,

To Mr. ——.   (———).

LETTER XLI.

Do. to a Publisher's firm.

Newcastle upon Tyne, May 3rd, 18—.

GENTLEMEN,—As our business is rapidly on the increase, we are desirous of opening an account with your house, and shall feel obliged by your transmitting us a trade list of your publications, as well as some of your general catalogues. Our usual terms of settlement are as follows (*here state them*). Should they be agreeable to your house, the favour of an early attention to our request will oblige,

Gentlemen,

Your obedient servants,

(—— and ——).

To Messrs. —— & Co.

LETTER XLII.

From a Friend in the country to a Friend in London.

York, Nov. 7th, 18—.

DEAR ——,—I shall have occasion, in the course of a few weeks, to pay a visit to the metropolis. Being almost a stranger there, and business being my principal object, I should wish to be as near the city as possible. The purport of my present letter to you, therefore, is to ask you to recommend me one of the houses at which travellers from the country, sojourning for a brief space in London, and having business in the city, can meet with accommodation. As you are sufficiently aware of my views and circumstances, to know what will suit me, I leave the selection to you; and trusting to hear from you soon,

I remain

Yours faithfully,

(————).

To ——, ESQ.

LETTER XLIII.

An Answer.

London, Dec. 15th, 18—.

DEAR ——, —I am delighted to hear that there is a chance of our seeing you again, and hope that you will at all events contrive to spend one or two evenings at our house during your stay.

As regards lodgings, you will find Mrs. ——'s a quiet, clean, and comfortable boarding-house, upon reasonable terms, and as it is at No. —, —— Street, I think it is a very convenient situation for what you require. Believe me,

Yours very truly,

To ——, Esq.   (————.)

———

LETTER XLIV.

From a friend in the country to one in London, with a Commission.

Manchester, June 6th, 18—.

DEAR——, —I have two small accounts due to me in London, but they are too trifling in amount to allow of my making a visit to the metropolis, to obtain payment of them. Will you, therefore, oblige me by permitting one of the persons in your house to call upon the parties, namely, Mr. ——, of —— street, and Mr. ——, of —— street, and ask for the several sums, the first amounting to ——, the second to ——. Should you obtain them, you can remit them to me by a post-office order, or in any other way you please. I shall be most happy to return the favour, should any opportunity occur of so doing.

I remain, dear Sir,

Yours faithfully,

(—— —.)

To ——, Esq.

———

LETTER XLV.

*From a Gentleman desirous of letting his house for a short
period, to a House-agent.*

London, Aug. 17th, 18—

Sir,—As myself and family intend to leave London for the
space of at least three months, my house, which is situated in
—— street, and is well furnished, will be empty, unless I can
meet with some person who is in want of accommodation during
that period.   I am disposed to let it at the very moderate rate
of £—— for the quarter ; and shall be prepared to give up
possession on ——. I shall, therefore, be glad to avail myself of
your professional assistance, trusting that you will make all
requisite inquiries as to the means, the character, and responsibility of any party with whom you may think it advisable to
come to terms.

I am, Sir,

Your obedient servant,

To Mr. ——.   (————).

LETTER XLVI.

An application for a Situation on the Railway.

Basingstoke, March 30th, 18—.

Sir,—Understanding that you are a shareholder in some of
the principal railways, and on intimate terms with several of
the directors, I venture to solicit your kind interest on behalf
of my eldest son, ——, now in his twenty-second year.   His
education has been of a useful character, and since he left
school, he has been articled to Mr. ——, the ——, of this town.
The period for which he was articled has expired, but my
means are insufficient to enable me to establish him in business.
Under these circumstances, I venture to write to you, in the hope
that, should you have it in your power to oblige me in his
behalf, by pointing out any situation that you think would
suit him, either at the principal station, or any other on the

line, you would kindly intercede in his favour. In doing so,
you would confer a lasting obligation both on him and me.

I remain, Sir,
Your obliged servant,

To —, Esq.   (———).

LETTER XLVII.

A hint for the Payment of a small Debt.

London, March 7th, 18—.

MY DEAR SIR,—Being at present rather short of ready cash,
I am compelled to remind you that I have in my possession
your I O U for the sum of £——. I need say no more, but that
I hope to hear from you, if convenient, by return of post, and
remain,

My dear Sir,
Yours, most sincerely,

To —, Esq.   (———).

LETTER XLVIII.

Another.

Canterbury, May 7th, 18—.

DEAR SIR,—I must remind you that I still hold your I O U
for the sum of £——, and hope you will give it early attention,
as I am just now much troubled for ready money.

Yours, very truly,

To —, Esq.   (———).

K

LETTER XLIX.

Another, more pressing.

Hull, June 10th, 18—

SIR,--I must again remind you of your promise to take up your I O U for the sum of £——, on the 15th of ——. Nothing but my really wanting the money would have induced me to be thus urgent, but I assure you that further delay will materially inconvenience

Yours most faithfully,

To ——.   (———).

LETTER L.

In Answer to the above.

Louth, June 12th, 18—.

DEAR SIR,—I am happy in being able to enclose you the sum for which I have been already too long your debtor. Assuring you that unforeseen disappointments have been the sole cause of any want of punctuality,

Believe me,
Dear Sir,
Your obliged and faithful servant,

To ——.   (———).

LETTER LI.

To a Correspondent, requesting the Payment of a sum of money.

York, April 12th, 18—.

SIR,—Although the balance of the account between us has been of long standing in my favour, yet I would not have applied to you at present, had not a very unexpected demand been made upon me for a considerable sum, which, without your assistance, it will not be in my power to answer. When I have an opportunity of seeing you, I shall then inform you of the nature of this demand, and the necessity of my discharging it. I hope you will excuse me this freedom, which nothing but a regard to my credit and family could oblige me

to take. If it does not suit you to remit the whole, part will
be thankfully received by

Your obedient servant,

To ——.   (———)

LETTER LII.

The Answer.

Chelsea, June 3rd, 18—.

SIR,—I have just received your letter, and am sorry to hear
of your inconvenience. The account between us would have
been sooner settled, but for the failure of two of my principal
creditors. I have just, however, received a remittance from
——, and am greatly pleased that it is in my power to answer
the whole of your demand. The balance between us is ——
pounds, for which I have sent inclosed an order on Mr. ——,
the banker. Hoping you will speedily surmount this difficulty,

I am,

Your sincere well-wisher,

To ——.   (———).

LETTER LIII.

Delaying the Payment of a Debt.

13, Lowndes Street, Jan. 14th, 18—.

SIR,—I really must beg of you to defer the settlement of
your account till after the middle of next month, when I shall
be in a condition to meet your demand. Regretting that circumstances prevent my being more prompt in attending to your
wishes,

I remain, Sir,

Your obedient servant,

To Mr. ——   (———).

LETTER LIV.

On the same subject to a Firm.

Glasgow, June 15th, 18—.

GENTLEMEN,—I much regret that circumstances prevent my being as punctual as is my wont, and hope you will kindly renew the acceptance you hold of mine for another three months. The failure of a person largely indebted to me, and some other losses in business, have caused me severe inconvenience, and I really must depend upon your leniency as one means to enable me to recover myself.

        I remain,
            Gentlemen,
                Your obedient and faithful servant,

To Messrs. ——.   (————).

LETTER LV.

Enclosing an Instalment.

Bridge Street, Liverpool, Jan. 15th, 18—.

GENTLEMEN,—I herewith inclose the first half of a ten-pound note as an instalment towards your bill. I much regret that I am unable to send you the remaining seven pounds twelve shillings, but hope I shall be enabled to do so speedily. The long credit I am compelled to give frequently occasions me the greatest difficulty, and compels me to put others to inconvenience where I feel most unwilling to do so.

        I remain,
            Gentlemen,
                Your obliged and faithful servant,

To Messrs. ——.   (————).

LETTER LVI.

In Reply.

London, Jan. 16th, 18—.

DEAR SIR,—We duly received your instalment, and shall be happy to wait for the remainder until the 4th day of February,

when we trust your circumstances will enable you to meet it.
Meanwhile, we shall be quite willing to continue our transactions with you as usual.

> We are,
> Deaɪ Sɪɪ
> Youɪ ɔbedient and faithful servants,

To **Mr** ——. (———) aɑd (———).

LETTER LVII.

Urging Payment.

London, 15th February, 18—.

Sɪʀ,—In consequence of my having a heavy sum to make up
by the ——th, I must beg you to give immediate attention to
my account, which has already run far beyond my usual extent
of credit. You have not remitted me anything for —— months,
and I must really urge greater promptness on your part, as the
nature of my business does not allow me to remain out of mɣ
capital so long.

> I am, Sir,
> Your cbedient servant,

To Mr. ——. (———).

LETTER LVIII.

In Answer.

London, Feb. 16th, 18—.

Sɪʀ,—I am really grieved to have occasioned you any inconvenience, but I assure you that the depression of business of
late has had a similar effect upon the incomes of professional
men, and I have scarcely known which way to turn to extricate
myself from the difficulty.

If you will kindly wait about three or four weeks longer, I
think I can safely promise you —— pounds, and the rest of **your**

account within a few months after. Again regretting that I
cannot at once meet your wishes,

I remain, Sir,
Yours faithfully,

To Mr. ——.   (———).

LETTER LIX.

For a Loan.

4, Curry Street, June 14th, 18—.

DEAR ——,—I write to ask you a rather disagreeable favour.
In consequence of imprudently placing my name to one of ——'s
bills, I find that I am likely to be involved in some expense and
difficulty, if I cannot at once meet the amount. Would you,
under these circumstances, accommodate me with the loan of
—— pounds until dividend day, when I shall be able to return
it without fail. It vexes me much to ask a friend such a thing,
but you will, I hope, excuse it on the part of

Yours, most truly,

To ——, Esq.   (—— ——).

LETTER LX.

The Answer.

Chelsea, June 15th, 18—.

DEAR ——,—I inclose you the sum you require, and to which
you are heartily welcome. Only, my dear fellow, do take one
piece of friendly advice—never touch paper where money is
concerned, unless it be a bank-note. I have been "bitten" so
often in that way myself, that I would rather lend a man
money on his plain word of honour than see my name bandied
about among Jews and scamps of every description. Trusting
that you will take what I say in good part,

Believe me,
Yours, very sincerely,

To ——, Esq   (———)

LETTER LXI.

Soliciting a Loan from an intimate Friend.

London, March 16th, 18—.

MY DEAR SIR,—A disappointment in the receipt of some money due has exposed me to a temporary embarrassment. The sum which would extricate me from this painful difficulty, is not large, as £—— would be amply sufficient to release me from my present pressure. I have so great an aversion to borrowing money from professional lenders, that I prefer the course of soliciting the aid of some well-known friend. I have thought of several, but of none with a greater degree of confidence than yourself, with whom I have been, during so many years, upon terms of the warmest intimacy. Can you grant me, then, the accommodation of the above sum, without in any way entrenching on your own convenience? If you can, I believe I may rely on your readiness to do so; and you may in turn depend upon it being reimbursed with the strictest punctuality by the —— of ——. A speedy reply to this request will extremely oblige,

My dear Sir,

Yours most sincerely,

To ——, Esq.   (———).

LETTER LXII.

In Answer to the above, affirmatively.

March 17th, 18—.

MY DEAR SIR,—I have just received your letter, soliciting the loan of £——, and it gives me much pleasure that I have it in my power to be able to accommodate so old and valued a friend. I therefore lose no time in forwarding you a cheque upon Messrs. —— for the above sum, in reimbursing which I beg you will suit your own convenience, and thereby oblige

Your old and

Very sincere friend,

To ——, Esq.   (———)

LETTER LXIII.

In Answer to the above, on account of incapability.

Saturday, March 17th, 18—.

MY DEAR SIR,—While I readily acknowledge the claim you have upon my friendship, and while I feel that there is no one whom I should be more willing, or be prouder to oblige than yourself, I am sure you will not think that I am capable of deception, when I declare that I am myself in difficulty for ready cash, and that, however willing to befriend you, I have it not in my power to comply with your request. Hoping that you may be more successful in some other quarter, and with feelings of regret at my own inability to render you a service which you might otherwise readily command,

Believe me to remain,

Ever your sincere friend,

To ——, Esq.   (———).

LETTER LXIV.

Declining to lend money.

Battersea, March 3rd, 18—.

MY DEAR ——,—I have always made it a principle in life never to borrow or lend money, not even when members of my own family have been concerned.   I therefore trust you will excuse conduct which may seem harsh and uncourteous on my part, but which I have ever found to be the safest, and, in the long run, the kindest course for all parties.

I remain,

My dear ——,

Yours very faithfully,

To ——, Esq.   (———).

LETTER LXV.

The same, on the score of inability.

MY DEAR ——,—If there is any one in the world I should be willing to oblige in any way, it is yourself; but, unhappily, I am at this moment so driven for funds that I last week was compelled to borrow five pounds to make up my workmen's wages on Saturday night. Under this state of things, I know you will take the will for the deed, and, sincerely hoping you may meet with help elsewhere,

Believe me,

Yours ever truly,

To Mr. ——.   (———)

LETTER LXVI.

Application for a Loan on Insurance.

Chelsea, June 4th, 18—.

GENTLEMEN,—Having been insured in your office for —— years to the amount of —— £, at —— £ ,, s. premium, I wish to know what sum you would feel disposed to advance me thereupon, as I am anxious to complete a partnership in business for my eldest son.

The favour of an early communication will oblige,

Gentlemen,

Your obedient servant,

(———)

To the Managers and Directors of the
        —— Insurance Office

LETTER LXVII.

An application for Shares in a Building (or other) Society.

Throgmorton Place, City Road, July 12th, 18—.

SIR,—I beg that you will place my name on the list of share-holders in the —— society for —— shares at the rate of ——, and herewith inclose a cheque for —— as the first instalment payable thereupon.

I am, Sir,

Your obedient servant,

To the Secretary of the —— Society.   (———)

LETTER LXVIII.

To transfer Shares.

Chertsey, Nov. 15th, 18—.

SIR,—In answer to your application respecting shares in the ——, I beg to say that I shall be happy to transfer (*mention the number*) to you, and if you will give your solicitor the requisite directions, the necessary forms shall be prepared immediately.

> I am, Sir,
> Your obedient servant,

To ——, Esq.   (———).

————

LETTER LXIX.

An invitation to a bachelor-party.

Sept. 11th, 18—.

MY DEAR ——,—Myself, and half a dozen other good fellows, are going to devote a few hours on —— evening to the enjoyment of a few glasses of wine, chit-chat, and so on. I hope you will make one, as we have not enjoyed the "feast of reason and flow of soul" in each other's company for some time past

> Believe me,
> Dear ——,
> Yours ever,

To ——, Esq.   (———)

————

LETTER LXX.

An invitation to a private dinner.

Clarendon Square, Nov 12th, 18—.

DEAR ——,—My old friend —— is coming to take a chop with me on ——, the —th, and I hope you will come and join

us at six o'clock. I know you are not partial to large parties,
so trust you will think us two sufficient company.

Yours ever truly,

To ——, Esq.   (———).

LETTER LXXI.

An invitation to a water party.

July 12th, 18—.

DEAR ——,—Jack ——, myself, and four others are going
down to Richmond in a six-oared boat next ——. Now, you are
a jolly fellow, and a good steersman, so I hope you will give us
your company and your services; indeed, we will take no excuse. We shall set out from my lodgings at —— o'clock,
without fail.

Yours truly, in haste,

To ——, Esq.   (———).

LETTER LXXII.

An invitation to a pic-nic party.

London, July 3rd, 18—.

MY DEAR SIR,—We are endeavouring to get up a small excursion to visit —— on the —— of this month. Will you do
us the favour of making one of our number? Mrs. —— and
my family desire their compliments, and request me to mention
that they have taken upon themselves the task of providing the
" creature comforts" for that occasion, and trust that their
exertions will meet with unanimous approval. Should you
have no previous engagement for that day, and feel disposed to
join our party, a carriage will be at your door by —— o'clock
on —— morning; and believe me to be,

My dear Sir,
Yours most sincerely,

To ——, Esq.   (———).

P.S.—The favour of an early answer will oblige.

LETTER LXXIII.

Another, to a Father of a Family.

London, July —, 18—.

MY DEAR SIR,—May I hope that you will allow your boys and girls to join mine in an excursion to —— on the ——? We expect to make a rather large party, and have, therefore, made arrangements to dine at ——.

In haste, believe me,

My dear Sir,

Yours ever sincerely,

To ——, Esq.   (———)

LETTER LXXIV.

Another, from one Single Man to Another.

London, Aug. 15th, 18—.

DEAR ——,—I am commissioned by Mrs. —— to press you into the service for a pic-nic to ——. You are requested to bring your cornopean, as —— has volunteered to bring one or two who do a little in the musical way. Mind, the —th is the day, for you always forget. So no more at present from

Yours ever,

To ——, Esq.   (———)

LETTER LXXV.

From a Brother to his married Sister in a foreign country, or in one of the Colonies.

London, June 3rd, 18—.

MY DEAR SISTER,—We have been long impatiently expecting a letter from you. The last we received was far too brief, as we were anxious to know more about the particulars of your voyage, and how you managed on your arrival at the place of destination. The distance which now separates us invests all that concerns you with a peculiar interest, and our anxiety on the subject of your welfare can only be allayed by as full and particular a recital as you can possibly write. Believe me, it is no mere curiosity that elicits this wish on our part to be better informed of all that befalls you; as, since we have but too much reason to conclude that our meetings together are perhaps now for ever closed, we are the more anxious to hear from you as often as possible, and I am sure you will not withhold from us this pleasure. As for ourselves at home, little change has taken place since you left England; the health of our dear parents remains much the same; as does also that of most of our relatives and connections. They all unite with me in wishing you and your husband all possible health and happiness, and I remain,

My dear Sister,

Your affectionate brother,

To Mrs. ——. (———).

LETTER LXXVI.

From a Brother in the country to his Sister in London.

Gloucester, September 4th, 18—.

MY DEAR SISTER,—Not having heard from you for the last ——, I feel anxious to learn how you are at present situated, and what may be your future prospects. You have now been nearly three years with Mrs. ——, and the period for which you were articled to that lady draws to a close. I hope you have now formed some plan for the future; and whatever that plan may be, I shall, if you think proper to confide in me, be most willing and ready to give you my best advice and assistance. If you purpose having a short rest from business, and will come down to —— for a few weeks, your sister-in-law, who unites with me in the kindest regards to you, will do her best to make that period pass agreeably. Pray write quickly to

Your affectionate brother,

To Miss Sarah ——. (———)

LETTER LXXVII.

From a young Man in the gold countries to his Parents in London.

Bear Island, Nov. 13 h, 18—.

MY DEAR PARENTS,—It is with more than pleasure that I write to acquaint you not only with my safe arrival, but that I am (as I hope you and all at home are) in excellent health and spirits.

We started, as you know, from —— on the ——; but had so rough a passage, that we did not reach Port —— till ——; but, thank God, without much illness on board, except the usual sea-sickness. I was fortunate in immediately getting employment as a ——; which was, indeed, lucky, as my slender stock of money was exhausted, and everything is dear beyond belief. To be sure, it is a land of money, but money goes very little way, and I have not yet had the good luck to meet with one of the " nuggets," about which the whole world are talking. Indeed, I do not like the gold-diggers, as far as I have seen them, and while I can make —— per week by ——, I think I shall keep to the slow and sure style of work, and trust to industry and God's blessing to make enough to keep me in plenty and respectability.

However, I have done sufficiently well to be able to send over (*name the sum*), which will be punctually paid to you by ——, to whom I have entrusted this letter. Hoping soon to be able to do much more for you, who have worked so hard to bring up me and my brothers and sisters, believe me, with kindest love to all relations and friends,

Your affectionate Son,

To ——.   (——).

LETTER LXXVIII.

Another.

Dog Quarry, Dec. 4th, 18—.

DEAR ——,—We are getting on famously, far better than at home, and I should advise every one who cannot get either work, or proper payment for it, to join us at ——. To be sure, it is a rough life, and some of the characters you meet with require a little caution. Nor can I say much for the climate down here, but it is better in some other parts towards ——. Having, as you know, a little capital to start with, we have done very well; indeed, we have doubled our stock, and soon hope to leave the dangers and uncertainties of gold-digging and washing, and lead a quiet life as farmers or sheep-squatters. My advice to you, is to purchase (*enumerate articles*), which are a safe investment down here, and will fetch three times their value, and join us as soon as possible. Knowing your health and habits, I have no doubt you will be satisfied with Australia, although we are forced to rough it a little.

Hoping that less than a twelvemonth may see us as often together as we used to be on the other side of the ocean, believe me,

> My dear ——,
>
> Ever truly and sincerely yours,
> To ——.   (——).

LETTER LXXIX.

From a young Man in the gold diggings to his Sweetheart in ——.

Portland Town, Jan. 13th, 18—.

MY DEAREST ——,—At length, by the blessing of Providence, I am able to reclaim my promise, and claim you as the partner of my joys and sorrows for life.

I trust, from your constant affection when we both saw nothing but want and distress before us, that the news of my prosperity will be most acceptable to you. Never can I be sufficiently thankful to Mrs. Chisholm for the help her kindness procured me, but I shall feel far, far more grateful when I welcome my dearest —— to a home on this side of the wide ocean.

I send you ——, which will be amply enough for your outfit, also ——, which pray give to your mother with my most affectionate duty, and tell her, that, however far removed from her presence, neither you nor myself will ever forget, that, now we

have the power, it is our bounden duty to assist and cherish
her declining years.

I also send some little presents, chiefly of the produce of the
country, as tokens of friendship to —— (*mention the names*).
And now, with kindest love to all, and with heartfelt wishes
for your safe voyage and speedy arrival,

> Believe me,
>> Dearest ——,
>>> Your affectionate and impatient

To ——   (—— ——).

LETTER LXXX.

From a Person in a distant Colony, to his Friend in London.

Newfoundland, October 18th, 18—.

MY DEAR OLD FRIEND,—I believe I may now say that myself, Mrs. W——, and our two boys are comfortably housed.
We have had much to contend with, and a good deal of up-
hill work to encounter, but we now hope that brighter prospects
are dawning, and that we shall very soon find ourselves in a
state of comparative comfort.

When we arrived here, we were obliged to obtain shelter
where we could. House-rent is very high. For a house of
four rooms, constructed of wood, and all on the ground-floor,
from forty to fifty pounds a year is asked. A similar house in the
environs of London would not let for more than fifteen or six-
teen. Clothes, also, are very dear. A good coat will cost from
six to ten pounds, and other articles of clothing are in like
proportion. On the other hand wages are high, and employment plentiful, at least among the useful class of mechanics.
Most articles of food are cheap, the best beef and mutton
three-pence to four-pence per pound. Now and then we have
a change of kangaroo flesh, and a nice pie made of young
parroquets, and very nice eating they are, I assure you.

Sheep-feeding here is extensively pursued, and the quantity
of wool exported to England, as well as to other places, is fast
increasing. We also grow more corn than we consume, so that
in a few years, we shall become, like New South Wales, an
exporting country.

Mrs. W—— joins in kind regards to you and our friends in old England; to every one of whom we wish better days and happier prospects.

> I remain,
>> Dear friend,
>>> Yours very truly,

To Mr. ——. (————).

———

LETTER LXXXI.

Soliciting subscriptions to a W⟨...⟩

London, May 5th, 18—.

SIR (or MADAM),—May I venture to trespass on your kindness by soliciting the favour of your name in addition to the inclosed list of subscribers to a forthcoming work? I venture to hope that it will be of sufficient interest to merit your patronage, should you be willing to accord it

> I have the honour to remain,
>> Sir (or Madam),
>>> Your very obedient and faithful servant,

To ——. (————).

———

LETTER LXXXII.

The same, but more familiarly.

London, May 6th, 18—.

DEAR ——,—May I venture to ask for your friendly assistance in an undertaking I have very much at heart, viz. the publication of a work on which I have been long engaged. (*Here state title and other particulars.*) You are well aware that the subject is one to which I have devoted much anxious study and research, and I should feel grieved at the thought of so much labour being thrown away.

I find, however, that the subject is of too exclusive a nature to suit the taste of London publishers, and I am therefore desirous of venturing on publishing it by subscription. You

L

will, I know, pardon my thus trespassing upon your kindness,
in asking you to give me your own name, and to mention the
matter to any friends whom you may think likely to feel an interest in the subject. Believe me,

Dear ——,

Yours most sincerely,

To ——, Esq.   (————).

———

LETTER LXXXIII.
The Answer.

Portland Place, May 8th, 18—.

DEAR ——,—Pray add my name to your list, and feel assured
of my best wishes for the success of an undertaking, for the
effectual carrying out of which your name and reputation are
sufficient guarantee.

With regard to my friends, there are few who I can depend
upon in such a matter; but I will certainly lay the matter before
them, and shall hope to gain a few more subscribers to what is
at once a difficult and an important undertaking.

With reiterated wishes for your success,

Believe me,

Dear ——,

Ever truly yours,

To ——, Esq.   (————).

———

LETTER LXXXIV.
Application for subscription to a Charity.

Chelsea, October 8th, 18—.

SIR (or MADAM),—I take the liberty of inclosing a pros-
pectus of an institution which is likely to have a most beneficial effect upon the condition of the poor in our neighbourhood. (*Here state particulars.*) From your well-known liberality, I trust you will excuse this appeal from a stranger in
furtherance of an act of benevolence, and remain,

Sir (or Madam),

Your most obedient servant,

(————).

To ——.   ———

LETTER LXXXV.

The Answer.

London, October 20th, 13·—.

SIR,—I shall gladly contribute my mite towards the bene-volent design you advocate, and herewith inclose a cheque for ——. Wishing all success to so well intended a design,

Believe me,

Yours most faithfully,

To ——, Esq.　　　　　　　　　　　　(———).

LETTER LXXXVI.

A Note, declining.

London, October 20th, 18—.

MR. —— presents his compliments to Mr. ——, but regrets that, in consequence of many similar claims upon his purse, he is unable to contribute to a design, the excellence of which he fully recognises.

To ——, Esq.

LETTER LXXXVII.

On behalf of a sick person.

Blackwall, June 8th, 18—.

HONOURED SIR,—Understanding that you possess some in-terest in the —— hospital for ——, I venture to write to solicit your assistance on behalf of my son (*or* daughter, nephew, friend, &c., *as the case may be*), who has been for some time afflicted with —— (*state complaint or accident*). My own employ-ment does not produce enough to enable me to furnish him (*or* her) with the medical attention or the comforts required by a sick person, and the favour of your interest in procuring his admission into ▾ —— would be esteemed a lasting obligation by

Honoured Sir,

Your obedient humble servant,

To ——, Esq.　　　　　　　　　　　　(———).

LETTER LXXXVIII.

To a Governor of a public Free School.

Hoxton, September 6th, 18—.

SIR, — Understanding that you possess some influence among the Board of Directors of —— school, I beg to solicit your interest for my son ——, who is recommended by —— and ——, both, I believe, gentlemen well known to you. Having a family of —— children, their education is necessarily a source of great expense and anxiety, and I assure you that any assistance rendered towards achieving that end will be most thankfully acknowledged and gratefully remembered by,

Sir,

Your obedient and faithful servant,

To ——, Esq.   (————)

LETTER LXXXIX.

To delay the Payment of a bill.

New Street, August 7th, 18—.

SIR,—Your account, amounting to £——, has indeed remained some time unsettled, but disappointments of a pecuniary nature, to which I need not more particularly allude, will prevent my liquidating it for some time to come, perhaps three months, but the payment will not exceed that period. From the pressing language of your application, I am disposed to think that a promissory note for that time may be of service to you, in being negotiable; if so, I have no objection to give it and will be prepared to honour it when duly presented.

I am, Sir,

Your obedient servant,

To Mr. ——   (————).

LETTER XC.

A Gentleman desiring the Renewal of a Note of Hand.

London, August 3rd, 18—.

SIR,—My note of hand (or acceptance) will be due on the 28th instant, but I regret to say that, owing to circumstances beyond my control, I fear that I shall not be able to meet it. May I therefore request that you will grant me the indulgence of a short renewal of (six weeks), when I doubt not of my means to take it up. Your compliance with this wish will confer an obligation upon,

Sir,
Your very obedient servant,

To Mr. ——. (————).

LETTER XCI.

From a Tenant to a Landlord, excusing delay of Payment.

London, June 12th, 18—.

SIR,—I have now been your tenant above ten years in the house where I now live, and you know that I never failed to pay my rent quarterly when due. At present I am extremely sorry to inform you, that from a variety of recent disappointments, I am under the necessity of begging that you will indulge me one quarter longer. By that time I hope to have it in my power to answer your just demand, and the favour shall be ever gratefully acknowledged by

Your obedient humble servant,

To ——, Esq. (————)

LETTER XCII.

From a country Farmer, on the same occasion.

Cheshire, Sept. 18th, 18—.

HONOURED SIR,—I am extremely sorry that through a variety of unforeseen accidents, I am obliged to write to you on such a subject as this. The season last year was bad, but I was enabled to pay you. The present one has turned out much worse, and it being so long before we could get the corn home, it is not yet fit to be sold. I only beg your patience for about two months longer, when I hope to pay you faithfully, with gratitude.

                    I am, Sir,
                            Your honest tenant, and humble servant,
    To ——, Esq.   (————).

LETTER XCIII.

From a young Person in trade to a wholesale Dealer, who had suddenly made a demand on him.

                                York Street, June 15th, 18—.

Sir,—Your demand coming very unexpectedly, I must confess I am not prepared to answer it. I know the stated credit in this article used only to be four months; as it has been always the custom to allow, at least, two months more, I did not think you would have sent for it till that time, and, consequently, trusted to a practice so long established in trade. Sir, I beg you will not suppose it is any deficiency which hinders me from complying with your request, nor shall I ask any more than is usual. If you will be pleased to let your clerk call this day three weeks for one-half of the sum, it shall be ready, and the remainder in a fortnight after. Sir, you may take my word with the greatest safety, that I will pay you as I have promised; and if you have any reason to demand the money sooner, be pleased to let me know, that if I have it not, I may borrow it; for if I have lost credit with you, I hope I have not done so with all the world.

                    I am, Sir,
                            Your humble servant,
    To Mr. ——.   (————).

LETTER XCIV.

After meeting at a party.

York Hotel, February 18th, 18—.

MY DEAR MADAM,—I venture to address you on a subject of serious importance to my future happiness—at least, if I have not totally mistaken the impression created on my meeting with you last night at ——. Your lively good sense persuades me that the language of flattery would be far from pleasing, and I will not, therefore, wound your feelings by addressing to you compliments as unnecessary as they are inexpressive.

But I must entreat your pardon at the somewhat bold address I am about to make, and trust that its apparent presumption may be mitigated by the consideration that my own feelings are so deeply enlisted in its success or failure. You might, perhaps, have observed that my attentions were directed to you in a manner sufficiently marked to prove that some more than ordinary feeling directed them, and,—if I do not wholly mistake,—those attentions did not appear to be disagreeable to yourself. Impelled by this flattering and pleasing belief, I make bold to crave for the honour of being permitted a further acquaintance with one for whom I have formed so great an esteem.

I trust that the nature of our introduction will be sufficient warrant for my character and position, and that I may experience a renewal, ere long, of the delightful hours spent in your company. I shall, of course, make direct application to your (*father, mother,* &c.), should I receive your kind permission so to do; but I could not think of doing so, unless I felt persuaded that such a step would be agreeable to your own wishes. I need scarcely add anything more than entreat for the favour of an early reply, anxiously awaiting which,

I have the honour to be,

——

Your most faithful and devoted servant,

To ——. (————).

——

LETTER XCV.

Another.—To an acquaintance of longer standing.

Chelsea, October 15th, 18—.

MY DEAR MISS ——,—I have so long enjoyed the happiness of being received as a welcome guest at your respected parent's house, that I write with the more confidence on a subject of most serious importance to my welfare.

From constantly meeting with you, and observing the thousand acts of amiability and kindness which adorn your daily life, I have gradually associated my hopes of future happiness with the chance of possessing you as their sharer. Believe me, dear Miss ——, this is no outbreak of boyish passion, but the hearty and healthy result of a long and affectionate study of your disposition. It is love, founded on esteem; and I feel persuaded that your knowledge of my own character will lead you to trace my motives to their right source.

May I, then, implore you to consult your own heart, and, should I not have been mistaken in the happy belief that my feelings are in some measure reciprocated, to grant me permission to mention the matter to your parents.

Believe me, dear Miss ——,

Your ever sincere, but at present anxious friend,

To Miss ——.   (————)

LETTER XCVI.

On receiving a favourable answer.

Chelsea, October 16th, 18—.

DEAREST MISS (*or use Christian name*),—Words cannot express my delight on finding your note on my table last night. The toils of the day were over, but how delightful was it to find a letter—and *such* a letter!—from one whom I may now hope to hail as the companion of my whole future life! The weight taken off my mind by the candid and gentle confession of one whose love seemed too great a happiness to hope for is beyond description. To-morrow I shall hasten to the presence of her from whom I hope I may never henceforth be parted; but I could not retire to rest without making one feeble attempt to express my delight at finding that hopes so flattering have not been in vain.

Believe me, dearest,

Your devoted and happy lover,

To Miss ——.   (————)

LETTER XCVII.

To a Widow, from a Widower.

Queen's Square, Nov. 14th, 18—.

MY DEAR MADAM,—I am emboldened to lay open to you the present state of my feelings, being so convinced of your good sense and amiable disposition, that I feel assured you will deal candidly with me in your reply.

Like yourself, I have been deprived of the partner of my earlier life, and, as I approach the middle state of existence, I feel more and more the want of some kindred spirit to share with me whatever years are reserved to me by Providence. My fortune is such as to enable me to support a lady in the manner which I feel to be due to your accomplishments and position, and I sincerely hope that you will think carefully over my proposal; and, if you can make up your mind to share my fortune and affections, I trust that no efforts will be wanting on my part to ensure you the happiness you so well deserve.

I need scarcely say, that an early answer on a matter so much connected with my future happiness will be a great favour to,

My dear Madam,

Your devoted friend and admirer,

(————).

To Mrs. ——.

LETTER XCVIII.

To the Father of a Lady.

Upper Clapton, January 12th, 18—.

RESPECTED SIR,—I venture to hope that you will call all your friendly feelings to my assistance in considering a proposal I am about to lay before you, in which my happiness is much concerned.

For a long time past your daughter —— has held a strong hold over my affections, and I have reason to believe that I am not indifferent to her. My position is such as to warrant my belief that I could support her in the style of comfort which she so well deserves, and which it has been your constant aim to provide for your children. As regards my character and disposition, I trust they are sufficiently well known to you to give you confidence in the prospect of your child's happiness.

I have not, however, ventured on any express declaration of my feelings without first consulting you on the subject; as I feel persuaded that the straightforward course is always the best, and that a parent's sanction will never be wanting, when the circumstances of the case justify its being accorded.

Anxiously awaiting the result of your consideration on this important and interesting subject,

I remain, Sir,

Your most faithful and obedient servant,

(——).

To ——, Esq.

LETTER XCIX.

The Answer.

Lower Clapton, Jan. 14th 18—.

MY DEAR ——,—I thank you very much for the manly and honourable way in which you have addressed me in reference to my daughter's hand. I have long since perceived that your attentions to her were of a marked character, and that they appeared to give her much pleasure. I know no reason whatever to oppose your wishes, and, if I may judge from the manner in which she received the communication from myself, *you* will find a by no means unwilling listener.

Dine with us to morrow at ——, if you are not engaged, and you will then have an opportunity of pleading your own cause.

Meanwhile, believe me, with every confidence in your integrity
and good feeling,

Yours most sincerely,
(———).

To ——, Esq.

———

LETTER C.

Unfavourable, on account of a Pre-engagement.

Hammersmith, April 4th.

DEAR SIR,—It is always painful to return an unfavourable
answer, but such is unfortunately my task on the present
occasion.

My daughter has for a long time been engaged to a gentleman whose character and position give her no cause to regret
the tie.   At the same time she duly appreciates the compliment implied by your preference, and unites with me in the
sincere wish that, as an esteemed friend, you may meet with a
companion in every way calculated to ensure your happiness.

Believe me,
Dear Sir,
Your sincere friend,
(———).

To ——, Esq.

———

LETTER CI.

To a young Lady to whom one is engaged.

Chester, Oct. 15th, 18—.

MY DEAREST FANNY,—If there is one thing which can console
me for my unavoidable absence from your side, it is the pleasure of being able to pen a few lines to express, however feebly,
my continued and increasing affection for you.   It is, indeed, a
painful and irksome change from our rambles about the fields,
our evening duets, and our stolen conversations, to a dull routine
of mercantile accounts and the never-ending confusion of business.   Happily, however, my affairs are in a rapid state of
settlement, and I shall soon hope once more to bask in the

sunshine of my Fanny's sweet countenance, and to feed my imagination with thoughts of the happiness which her placid and sincere disposition will hereafter shed around a home! I need hardly say how eagerly I watch for the post, and how I cherish every line that bears the evidence of my dear girl's affection, and how gratefully every sentiment that flows from her pen is treasured in my memory.

God bless you, dearest Fanny, and believe me, with most respectful and affectionate remembrances to your parents, and all friends,

Your ever affectionate and devoted
(———).

To Miss ——.

LETTER CII.

Another, complaining of not receiving a letter.

DEAR ——,—Although temporarily estranged from the delights of your society, I cannot refrain from hoping that you will enable me to realise some slender happiness from a more frequent correspondence on your part. Four days have passed without my receiving a letter from you, and I am in painful anxiety lest illness should be the cause. Pray write quickly, or I shall really feel inclined to quarrel with you as an idle girl; nay, I shall absolutely grow jealous, and fancy that some more favoured suitor is undermining the affections of my dear girl.

But I have no fears. I too well know that your innate goodness of heart would prevent you trifling with the feelings of any one; so, hoping you will take this little scolding in good part, and relieve the offence by a very long letter as speedily as your fingers can write it,

Believe me,
Dear ——,
Your affectionate
(———).

To Miss ——.

LETTER CIII.

Another, on her birthday.

Ch. Ch. Oxford, Feb. 15th, 18—.

DEAREST JULIA,—How sad it is that I am hindered from being with you on this dearest of all days of the year—the day that gave my Julia to the light, and that laid the foundation of the greatest happiness of my life.

Words cannot express the deep gratitude I feel to that Power, which, in granting you life, has at the same time, year after year, ripened those graces of the soul as well as developed the outward perfections of the body. As I see you—the companion of my childish pains and pleasures, expanding into the woman who is to share both with me throughout my future lot, I feel almost surprised as to how I have deserved such happiness, and gratitude beyond expression to the kind parents who have encouraged and approved our affection.

Accept, dearest, the enclosed portrait. I feel that its original is too deeply stamped on your heart to require any effigy to remind you of him. It is, however, the most appropriate present I could offer to the cause of my happiness on this brightest of all days.

God grant that every succeeding year may see you increase in all that is charming in body and mind, and believe me,

Dearest Julia,

Your affectionate *husband,*

(————).

To Miss Julia ——.

LETTER CIV.

A Lover's quarrel.

Peter's St., Westminster, July 3, 18—.

MY DEAR ——,—It is with pain I write to you in aught that can seem like a strain of reproach, but I confess that your conduct last night both surprised and vexed me. Your marked approbation of the attentions paid to you by —— was as obvious as your neglect of myself. Believe me, I am in no way

given to idle jealousy—still less am I selfish or unmanly enough
to wish to deprive any girl on whom I have so firmly fixed my
affections, of any pleasure to be obtained in good society. But
my peace of mind would be lost for ever, did I believe that I
have lost one atom of your affection.

Pray write, and assure me that you still preserve your undivided affection for

Your devoted but grieved
(———).

To Miss ——

———

LETTER CV.

Explaining away an apparent slight.

August 5th, 18—.

MY DEAREST ——,—How grieved am I that you should think
me capable of wavering in my affection towards you, and
inflicting a slight upon one, in whom my whole hopes of happiness are centered! Believe me, my attentions to Miss ——
were never intended for anything more than common courtesy.
My long acquaintance with her father, and my knowledge of
her amiable character—as well as the circumstance of her being
a comparative stranger to the ——'s,—such were my sole reasons
for paying more attention to her than I might otherwise have
done.

Pray rest confident in the belief that my affection for you is
as unchanging as my regret is great that I should ever have
given you cause to doubt it, and believe me,

Dearest ——,

Yours ever sincerely and devotedly,
(———).

To Miss ——

———

LETTER CVI.

Warning a young Lady against an imprudent match.

12, King St., Nov. 6th, 18—.

MY DEAR MISS ——,—I have so much confidence in your good
sense and discretion, that I trust you will excuse me, as a very
old friend, offering a few words of advice to you on a matter
which may seriously affect the happiness of your whole life.

You are young, and have been unhappily bereft of parental
care for many years past. Under such circumstances you are
exposed to temptations, not only dangerous in themselves, ut
the more so, in proportion as your innocence of heart rend rs
you open and unsuspecting in your opinion of others.

Report seems to speak of —— as your accepted lover, or, at
all events, as having paid you of late many attentions which
appear to have been favourably received. I sincerely hope, my
dear Miss ——, that you will not feel offended at one who,
from long knowledge, entertains a father's feeling—almost a
father's anxiety—on your behalf, speaking plainly what he is
but too well aware of.

I have long had my eye upon young ——'s doings, and I am
convinced that, without saying anything unduly harsh, he is
not calculated to make any wife happy. He is violent and unre-
strained in his temper, extravagant in his habits, and by no
means particular as to the society he keeps. Believe me, my
dear child, you never could be happy with such a man. Your life
would be one of incessant suffering—you would find a tyrant to
whom you had enslaved yourself, not a protector and friend on
whom your weakness should depend for support—you would
perhaps find yourself neglected and forgotten, when the fleeting
charms of youth and beauty had departed, and you would find
yourself the victim of a man whose whole object is immediate gratification, but whose want of stability and decision of
character totally incapacitates him from looking forward to
the serious duties of the future. Think well of this, my dear
girl, and do not commit yourself by rashly encouraging the
advances of a young man of so doubtful a disposition. Reflect
upon the happy life your own parents enjoyed, and depend
upon it you will find that affection. unaccompanied by

esteem, is no incentive to linking your destinies with those of another.

And now, my dear girl, I close this long, and, it may seem, tedious lecture, trusting that God may lead you to weigh anxiously and carefully the consequences of so serious a step; and that your own heart may be your truest and soundest adviser, is the sincere prayer of,

Your affectionate guardian,

(————).

To Miss ——.

LETTER CVII.

To a young Lady from a young Tradesman.

London, Feb. 16th, 18—.

DEAR MISS ——,—Since I met with you at ——, my mind has been constantly filled with the remembrance of the pleasant moments passed in your society. My business has been improving of late, and, in point of prosperity, I have much cause to be thankful. But I feel that there are higher duties in life than can be fulfilled by a man in his single state, and I am anxious to find a companion for my future life. Such a companion, dear Miss ——, I venture to believe I have found in you, and my earnest hope is, that you may be willing to appreciate the affectionate regard of one, who, however humble is his present position, has every desire to elevate that position for your sake.

Without attempting to use fine language, or make a parade of sentiment, I hope you will accept these lines as conveying the plain and honest sentiments of one, who, in anxious expectation of your reply,

Remains,

Dear Miss ——,

Your most devoted servant,

(————).

LETTER CVIII.

To an early companion and playmate.

London, July 6th, 18—.

MY DEAR EMMY,—For I can only think of you—woman as you now are—as the "little Emmy" of the many happy days of childhood we have spent together. Can you make up your mind to listen to a very awful confession? In plain words, I love you as heartily now as ever, and, if I may judge from our last night's meeting after so long a separation, you have not quite lost the remembrance of your old playfellow. But, joking apart, Time has done much for both of us—for you, in making you all that can be desired by man as the object of his love and trust—for me, in enabling me to provide a home for her who has ever been dearest to me, and whose image has never faded from my memory amidst the varied exertions of a preliminary professional career.

And now, my dear Emmy, think well whether you can transfer that affection as a woman which, in your girlhood, was my chiefest delight. We shall meet on —— at ——'s, and then, perhaps, my heart may be gladdened by a belief that "there is something in first loves."

Eagerly awaiting our meeting,

Believe me,

Your affectionate old playmate and new lover,*

(————).

To Miss ——.

LETTER CIX.

From one young man to another in reference to an attachment.

Paddington, Jan. 3rd, 18—.

MY DEAR ——,—You will laugh at me, and with some reason, when I tell you that all my old scepticism about matrimonial

---

* This, and a few of the following letters, are given as specimens of the *naïve* and lively style of correspondence, which *intimate acquaintance* alone can justify the use of. Our readers must therefore be *cautious* in copying such examples.

M

happiness is at an end. I have met with a young lady, who, I believe, would convert even you to a belief that marriage may be a very happy state, and that bachelors are only miserable wretches after all.

In brief, I am the engaged and accepted suitor of Miss ——, whose —— you remember at ——. Words can scarcely suffice to express how great has been the enjoyment I have hitherto derived from her society, and, the more I see of her amiable character and high accomplishments, the more certain do I feel that the day which first made known to me her consent to share my fortunes, will prove one of the happiest in my whole existence.

You may think this a very wild effusion, and one strangely at variance with my former avowed callousness on the score of domestic life, but, believe me, you will soon be a convert, when you see my dear Louisa.

Wishing that you may prove as fortunate in the selection of a partner as I have at present reason to believe I myself am,

Believe me,
My dear ——,
Ever yours,
(————).

To ——, Esq.

————

LETTER CX.

The Answer.

Cambridge, Jan. 6th, 18—.

DEAR OLD FELLOW,—And so you really are to be a Benedict! Well! I have no objection, provided you feel convinced that it is a measure likely to tend to your happiness. For myself, I am still a bachelor, although I do not know what such temptation as you appear to have undergone might not do towards upsetting my present resolutions. You know I have no antipathy to matrimony, but, unlike yourself, I have not independent means sufficient to render me fearless of consequences, and should not be disposed to involve any woman whom I could like sufficiently to make my wife, in a doubtful state of circumstances—if not in a discomfort which must be painful to a man of proper feeling and honour. At the same time, believe me, I cordially sympathise with your delight at the prospect of an agreeable union, and wish sincerely that every happiness may be the result.

Ever truly yours,
(————).

To ——, Esq.

LETTER CXI.

*From a young Tradesman to a Lady he had seen in public.**

Henrietta Street, July 12th.

MADAM,—Perhaps you will not be suprised to receive a letter from a person who is unknown to you, when you reflect how likely so charming a face, combined with manners so amiable, may be to create impertinence; and I persuade myself that when you remember where you sat last night at the playhouse, you will not need to be told that this comes from the person who was just before you.

In the first place, madam, I ask pardon for the liberty I then took in looking at you, and for the still greater I now take in writing to you; but after this, I beg leave to say that my thoughts are honourable, and to inform you plainly who I am, without pretending to be any better off than is really the case. I keep a shop, madam, in Henrietta Street, and although I have been but two vears in trade, I have tolerable custom. I do not doubt but it will increase, and I shall be able to do something for a family. If your inclinations be not engaged, I should feel most proud of the honour of waiting on you; and in the meantime, if you please to desire any friend to ask my character in the neighbourhood, I trust you will not find it prejudicial to,

Madam,
Your humble servant,
(————).

To Miss ——.

* The above is a specimen of a style of letter too frequently sent, but we hope few of our readers will think of writing on such a subject, with no better title to acquaintance.

LETTER CXII.

*From a young Man, avowing a passion he had entertained for a length of time, fearful of disclosing it.**

London, Feb. 13th, 18—.

DEAR MISS ——,—It is with no small degree of apprehension, as to the manner in which you may receive the following avowal, that I take up my pen to address you;—but I have so long struggled with my feelings, that they have now got the better of my irresolution; and, throwing aside all hesitation, I have ventured, although alarmed at my own boldness in doing so, to lay open my whole heart before you. For months past I have been oppressed with a passion that has entirely superseded every other feeling of my heart—that passion is *love*—and *you*—*you alone* are the object of it. In vain have I endeavoured to drive the idea from my mind, by every art that I could possibly think of: in vain have I sought out every amusement that might have a tendency to relieve my mind from the bias which it has taken, but love has taken that firm hold of my whole soul, that I am unable to entertain but one idea, one thought, one feeling, and that is always yourself. I neglect myself, my business, and can neither hear nor see any one thing—but you bear the chief part therein. Believe me, I am sincere, when I assert, that I feel it totally impossible to live apart from you—when near you, I am in paradise—when absent, I feel in torture; this, I solemnly assure you, is a true description of the feelings with which my breast is continually agitated, and it remains only for you to give a reality to those hopes, or at once to crush them, by a single word; say but that word, and I am the happiest or the most miserable of mankind.

Yours, till death,

(————).

To Miss ——.

———

* On grounds of plain *common sense*, we should not recommend this or the following letter for imitation; but people *will* send such letters!

LETTER CXIII.

To a Lady.

Tunbridge, July 3rd, 18—.

DEAR MADAM,—I have been so harassed with love, doubt, distraction, and a thousand other wild and nameless feelings, since I had the happiness of being in your company, that I have been unable to form one sane reflection, or to separate events from the feelings that accompanied them—in fact, I have been totally unable to bring my thoughts into anything like regularity, for they are so entirely mixed up with the idea of yourself, that the business of the world, and the pursuits of amusement and pleasure, have been entirely forgotten in the one passion that holds undivided empire over my soul. I have deferred from day to day penning this confession to you, in order that I might have been enabled to have done so with some degree of ease and calmness; but the hope has proved fruitless. I can resist no longer, for to keep silent on a subject which is interwoven with my very existence, would be death to me. No, I am unable to do so, and I have therefore determined to lay open to you the sufferings of my heart, and to implore from you a restoration of that peace and happiness which once were mine. You, my dear Miss ——, are alone the cause of my unhappiness, and to you alone can I look for a relief from the wretchedness that has overwhelmed me. The fervent passion that devours my soul for your adorable self, can only be allayed by the declaration that I am loved as fervently in return. But dare I ask so much purity, so much sweetness, mildness and modesty, to make such a declaration?— I know not what I say—but O! my dear Miss ——, be merciful, and if you cannot *love* me—say, at least, that you do *not hate* me. Never could I survive the idea of being hateful to that angelic being, whose love I prize more than existence itself. Let me then cling to the idea that time may accomplish that which, I fain hope, a first impression has done resuming, unless a fatal pre-engagement exists (a thing I dare not trust myself to think of), that you will comply with my request, seeing that

my designs are perfectly sincere and honourable. I remain,
waiting with the utmost impatience for your favourable reply,

Dear Miss ——,

Your devoted servant till death,

(———).

To Miss ——

LETTER CXIV.

From a Lover to a Father on his attachment to the Daughter.

April 2nd, 18—.

SIR,—As I scorn to act in any manner that may bring
reproach upon myself and family, and hold clandestine
proceedings unbecoming in any man of character, I take the
liberty of distinctly avowing my love for your daughter,
and humbly request your permission to pay her my addresses, as I flatter myself my family and expectances will
be found not unworthy of your notice. I have some reason
to imagine, that I am not altogether disagreeable to your
daughter; but I assure you, honestly, that I have not as yet
endeavoured to win her affections, for fear it might be repug-
nant to a father's will.

I am, Sir,

Your most obedient servant,

(———).

To Mr. ——.

LETTER CXV.

The Father's answer in the negative.

Hackney, April 3rd, 18—.

SIR,—I make no doubt of the truth of your assertions,
relative to yourself, character, and connections; but as I think
my daughter too young to enter into such a serious engage-

ment, I request I may hear no more of your passion for the present; in every other respect,

I am, Sir,

Your most obedient,

(———).

To Mr. ——.

———

LETTER CXVI.

In the Affirmative.

SIR,—There is so much candour and honour apparent in your letter, that to withhold my consent would be both ungenerous and unjust. As the duty of a father demands, I shall first make some necessary inquiries, assuring you that I would never oppose my daughter's choice, except I had some very just reason to imagine it would be productive of ill consequences, for I am convinced that, in the marriage state, happiness consists only in reciprocal affection. You may therefore depend upon hearing from me in a few days; till then I remain,

Your very faithful servant,

(———).

To Mr. ——.

———

LETTER CXVII.

A Gentleman proposing a day for the nuptials.

London, August 3rd, 18—.

MY DEAR ——,—The happy day to which I have looked forward as the blissful reward of our mutual constancy is not far distant, if the proposal I am now about to make should meet the approbation of yourself and parents. It is this: that our nuptial ceremony may be performed on the —— of the present month, and in the parish church of ——. I hope to have the pleasure of seeing you soon; we can then give the subject a lengthened discussion; if, however, you should wish to write before we meet, you can mention briefly whether the day I have fixed will suit the convenience of yourself and family; and in

the hopes that I may claim shortly the privilege of signing
myself your affectionate husband,

Believe me for the present,

Your sincerest friend, and most attached,

To Miss ——.   (————).

LETTER CXVIII.

To a Lady, complaining of her coolness.

Eaton Place, June 10th, 18—

DEAR ——,—How often have I passed my late conduct in re-
view before me, endeavouring to discover by what word or act
I could have given you offence. Vain, however, has been the
attempt, for the offence which I have given must have been
totally inadvertent, and could never have sprung from any in-
tention to have given you even a moment's uneasiness. But
that by some means I have had the misfortune to incur your
displeasure, has been but too evidently indicated by the change
of your behaviour towards me, a change from the kindness of
an attached friend, to the cool indifference of a distant acquaintance. Of late, when in your presence, I have been
many times upon the point of asking upon what occasion, and
by what means, I have displeased you? But as constantly have
needed the courage to do so, and my voice has failed me,
whenever I have endeavoured to make the attempt. In the
hopes of being eased from a painful state of anxiety, I write
this letter, and trust that you will give me some explanation
on the subject referred to, either by an answer in your hand-
writing, or through your own lips, at our next meeting. But
whatever that reply may be, of this be assured, that my esteem
for you can never know a change, and that you will ever live
as a cherished object in the breast of him who now subscribes
himself,

Yours most affectionately and sircerely,

To Miss ——.   (————).

LETTER CXIX.

A Gentleman desirous of discontinuing his addresses.

Bayswater, June 5th, 18—.

DEAR ——,—Whatever may be your future lot in life, and whatever change may take place in your circumstances, of this be assured, if put to the test, in me you will find a steadfast friend, and one ever ready to protect your interests. I make this avowal from a deep feeling of respect, which long experience of your worth has implanted within me, but in doing so (and, believe me, it is a declaration that causes me inexpressible pain to utter), I have also to make another avowal, for which I apprehend you are little prepared, and which I fear may give some shock to your feelings. My dear ——, with pain I utter it,—I must resign all hopes of our future union. Ask me not wherefore: my answer would inflict an additional pang in the breasts of both. This is no hasty resolve; I have deliberately weighed it, and know it to be essential to our mutual happiness and welfare. Whatever letters I may have of yours, I will dispose of as you think fit; and if you prefer it will inclose them to you, under seal; entreating, however, that you will grant me the indulgence of being allowed to keep only one, as a memorial of the past; and with this request, I bid you a painful but affectionate adieu, and entreat you will believe me,

Ever yours sincerely,

To ——.   (——).

LETTER CXX.

A Man-Servant to the object of his affections.

London, May 13th, 18—.

DEAR ——,—How often do I think of those innocent and happy days when much of our time was passed together. Servitude has since separated us; but if I may judge of your heart by my own, our feelings of affection towards each other have not undergone the slightest change. Our attachment is the same, and we must both long for that period when, freed from servitude, the useful toils of our past life may meet their reward, a reward to consist in our union, and a comfortable settlement in some honest calling. You will be happy to hear that my present situation is one of much comfort; I have a kind and considerate master and mistress, my wages are sufficient to enable me to save half of them, which I very regularly place in the Savings' Bank, my duties are not oppressive, and a liberal board is provided for the servants. How do you fare in these particulars? I should be glad to hear, when next you write. For myself, you see, I have no cause of complaint, and the interest which I feel in your welfare bids me hope that your situation is one of equal comfort and convenience. If you can favour me with a few lines, I shall be most happy to receive them. Adieu for the present, and

Believe me to be,

Ever yours most affectionately,

To ——.   (————).

LETTER CXXI.

A Gentleman to his Daughter, on her preference of a Suitor.

Belle Vue Villa, December 3rd, 18—.

MY DEAR ——,—What pleasure must it give me when I declare that my children's conduct has ever displayed that dutiful affection, which has made their present happiness and future welfare my constant aim! To find that they have made a prudent choice in their partners for life, and to see them living in harmony, and in comfortable circumstances, with those partners, have been among my nearest and most cherished wishes. I suppose I shall occasion you some little emotion in mentioning the name of Mr. ——; but be assured, my dear child, that from my own observation of that gentleman's character and from the esteem in which he is generally held, there is scarcely one amongst my acquaintance for whom I have greater respect, and whom I regard, from his worldly position, his integrity, his gentlemanly conduct, his prudent and well-known good temper as being more likely to make a woman happy. I can therefore truly say, that although I shall sorely feel the loss of your dear company, I cannot but approve of the choice you have made;

and in regard to his visits in the character of a suitor, neither
I nor your mother will offer any obstacle. As you and Mr.
—— have preferred addressing me upon this subject, by letter,
I return my answer in the same form, and am,

My dear child,

Your ever affectionate father,

To ——   (————)

LETTER CXXII.

A Gentleman to his Son, on the marriage of the latter.

Doncaster July 11th, 18—.

MY DEAR ——,—It is with no small pleasure and with no
slight feelings of parental pride, that I now congratulate you
upon your recent change of state. That you have my best
and heartiest wishes for your future happiness you already
know, but I feel a natural pleasure in again giving them expression; and here I have to add, that no parent could join in
those wishes with more fervent sincerity than your dear and kind
mother, who desires you to unite with me in the most affectionate
regards to our new relation, our daughter-in-law. That your
marriage state may be blessed with the same domestic happiness that has fallen to my lot, is the sincere wish of,

My dear son,

Your ever affectionate father,

To ——   (————).

LETTER CXXIII.

From a Soldier ordered into active service.

Liverpool, June 3rd, 18—.

DEAR ——,—At length the dreaded time has arrived, which
is to separate us, perhaps for ever. God grant it may not be
so, but a soldier's life, my dear Mary, is very uncertain and
precarious. But believe me, amidst every danger and difficulty
of my career, I shall ever think fondly of our acquaintance,

and hope that a time may come when peace shall be restored, and when we shall be united as man and wife.

God bless you, my dear Mary, and believe me,

Your devoted lover,

To ——   (———)

LETTER CXXIV.

To his Parents after a victory.

Sevastopol, June 9th, 18—.

MY DEAR PARENTS,—I write in haste to you that we have just gained a glorious victory, though with considerable loss to ourselves. Wonderful to say, despite many narrow escapes during the terrific carnage and confusion, I have escaped without a wound of any sort. You will, I am sure, unite with me in rendering hearty thanks to God for this great mercy.

Our regiment is expected to start for —— on the ——th, but, as matters are comparatively quiet there, I hope that I may enjoy a speedy return home.

Give my dearest love to Susan and the children, and believe me,

Your delighted and thankful son,

To ——.   (———).

LETTER CXXV.

To a Physician in town.—Asking his advice.

Huddersfield, July 6th, 18 –

SIR,—For a long time past I have been suffering in the most distressing manner from a long train of symptoms which have baffled the skill of all the medical men down here, and which, I fear, if not arrested in their progress, will terminate in the total prostration of my strength. Loss of appetite, and desire of stimulating and artificial means of sustenance at irregular times, want of healthy sleep and consequent depression on rising in the morning, render life quite a burden to me, and interfere seriously with the discharge of my professional duties. I am of a florid complexion, slightly corpulent (*state description*

of appearance, habits, whether sedentary or active, &c., profes-
sion, and the hours it occupies, early habits, and any other
particulars you think may bear upon the matter.)

My friend Mr. ——, who has been staying here for a few days,
speaks in high terms of your treatment of him under similar
circumstances. As far as I can perceive, our constitutions, as
well as our complaints, are very similar, and so satisfied am
I of your professional repute, that I would gladly have paid a
visit to London to consult you in person; various reasons, however, render that impossible, and I therefore hope that you will
enter into a correspondence with me on the subject. Meanwhile, I beg to inclose a cheque for —— upon Messrs. ——, and
assure you that I shall think the restoration of my health more
than an equivalent for any sum it may cost me.

> I have the honour to remain, Sir,
> > Your very obedient servant,
> > > (————).

To Dr. ——.
Or to —— Esq., M.D., or M.R.C.S.

LETTER CXXVI.

Recommending a successor on retiring from business.

Manchester, June 3rd, 18—.
To Messrs. ——, ——, and Co.

GENTLEMEN,—We flatter ourselves that there are many
friends amongst our connection, who will regret to hear that
we are just upon the point of relinquishing business. In doing
so, our premises and stock of goods will be transferred to the
hands of Messrs. —— and Co., who will, in future, carry on
the business on the same approved system, and the same
extensive scale as ourselves, provided they can rely on receiving
the patronage of our connection; in the hopes of which it is our
pleasure and duty to present those gentlemen to your notice.
We cannot speak too highly of the confidence we feel in their
liberal mode of conducting business, and their strict attention
and punctuality in their mercantile transactions; and, in the

hope that they may be honoured with the same countenance received by ourselves from your respectable firm,

We beg to subscribe ourselves,

Your obliged and most obedient servants,

(———— and Co.).

LETTER CXXVII.

A Tradesman proposing his Son as an apprentice.

London, Feb. 14th, 18—.

SIR,—As I understand from —— that you have a vacancy for an apprentice, I am anxious to place my son under your charge, in order that he may acquire a competent knowledge of your business, which he seems to be strongly inclined to follow in preference to any other. I know not what your terms may be, but if moderate, I shall have no objection to complying with them, and, with the view of settling that point, shall be happy either to receive a note from you on the subject, or to meet you at your own, or my house, when we can enter into full particulars. Allow me to add, that my son has received a good plain education, fully adequate to all the usual requirements of a man of business, and that I think you would find him of a cheerful and pliant disposition, of industrious habits, and both quick and willing to receive instruction.

I am, Sir,

Your very obedient servant,

To Mr. ——   (————).

LETTER CXXVIII.

A Parent's answer to a young Woman in place.

Barnstaple, February 6th, 18—.

To OUR DEAR ——,—Your letter, which we duly received, did indeed comfort our hearts; for notwithstanding our reliance on your prudence and virtue, yet your youth and inexperience filled us with an anxiety which none but parents know. Thank God, you are in a place, and one that is likely to be comfortable

We need not give you much advice concerning your duty; your 'good sense will dictate to you what is right.

We all miss you so much. Your brothers and sisters are often talking about you, and wondering what Elizabeth is employed about just then. As for poor William Kelly, he cannot hear your name mentioned without tears coming into his eyes, which he hastily wipes away, as if ashamed of them. Why did you not mention him in your letter? He thought it unkind. You say you cannot love him; yet surely you must esteem his kindness, his industry, and good qualities.

Well, dear girl, we will leave this to time. You are far too young to unite yourself to any one for the present; and we do not fear your forming an engagement without seeking the counsel of your parents; but, no doubt, whenever that happens we shall approve of your choice.

Nothing particular has occurred among our friends and neighbours since you left.

But all friends desire to be kindly remembered, William Kelly in particular. We have now nothing more to add, but our blessing; and that God Almighty may bless and preserve you, is the prayer of

Your affectionate parents,

To ——. (———).

LETTER CXXIX.

From a young Man in the country to a young Woman in service in London.

Barnstaple, February 18th, 18—.

DEAR ——,—You did not, it is true, give me liberty to write o you, neither did you decidedly forbid it; therefore, although I cannot flatter myself that hearing from me will give you anything like the pleasure which a letter from you would give me, yet I trust that you are not altogether indifferent towards me. That you esteem me as a friend, you have often told me; may I hope that this will ripen into a warmer feeling? You know how truly and solely my heart is yours, and how delighted I should be, if you would accept me as a lover, and, when cir-

cumstances would permit, as your husband. Think and
examine yourself, dear Elizabeth, before you answer me decidedly; for although you would be to me the greatest earthly
blessing if I had your love, yet, believe me, I could not wed
you, if you felt indifferent. My family and my circumstances
are well known to you. Being both brought up in the same
place, what is known to one is almost as well known to the
other. I am not rich, it is true; but I am able and quite willing to work, and I have every reason to suppose I shall succeed
in my business.

And now may I beg, as I do expect—or rather wish—a
favourable answer from you? That you will be candid and
sincere, I know; do be kind also, and gratify one who is

      Truly and affectionately yours,

To ——.   (———).

LETTER CXXX.

From an old Labourer to his Son.

       Bampton, January 22nd, 18—.

DEAR ——,—It is but little that I have used my pen for some
time past, and I feel in doing so somewhat strange; but I avail
myself of the cheap postage to write a few lines to you: not
doubting but that you will be glad to hear from us.

During the late winter, I was laid up with the rheumatism;
but, I am thankful to say, I have now recovered. Your dear
mother is well and hearty, and almost as active as a young
woman, and so cheerful and good too. Ah, dear Fred! 1 wish
you may be as fortunate in the choice of a partner as I have
been; you will then have cause to rejoice throughout life, however long your days may be spared. By what I hear of the
young woman you have chosen, yours is likely to be a happy
match also: use your endeavours, and I have no doubt it will
prove so.

In nine instances out of ten of unhappy marriages, I verily
believe it is the man's fault. I have known many working
men spend out of their scanty earnings two or three shillings a
week at the alehouse, and then complain that their homes are

not comfortable, and that their wives are peevish and cross. I have no patience with such fellows! I hope that you, my son, will keep away from public-houses and skittle-alleys, and such places of ruinous amusement. Heaven knows, that out of the poor man's hard earnings nothing can be squandered, without pinching the belly, or making the back to suffer for it. It is most unmanly to make our lot still worse by our own bad conduct.

I am thus pressing on this point to you, because I know that you are rather of a gay turn, and fond of company; therefore the more likely to be drawn into their fatal snare. Yet I would not have you morose; only keep your gaiety within due bounds; seek comfort where every man and woman ought to seek it, and where it is most to be found, by your own fireside. Take this advice as it is given, in kindness, and may it sink deep into your heart.

From your affectionate father,

To ——.   (————).

LETTER CXXXI.

From a farm-house.

Radford, Essex, 13th ——, 18—.

My DEAR SON,—I write a few lines, agreeably to your request, although I have but little news to communicate, beyond the usual doings of a farm-house, and those you know well enough. The crops are looking well, but rents are heavy, and I look forward to quarter-day with some anxiety. Our old horse, Dobbs, died yesterday. He has been for a long time fit for but little, but he was so old a favourite, that I could not find it in my heart to have him shot. The other live stock, including your favourite pigeons, are doing well, but we have missed several chickens of late, and I am going to set some traps, as I suspect that a fox has got through a hole in the palings just behind the water-butt.

I hope you are doing well, and that you will drive a good bargain with —— about ——. In these hard times, a man must have his eyes wide open and must look twice at a shilling before he spends it, otherwise there is no chance for him. But I know you are both a sharp lad, and a steady one, so I have no fear of your going wrong.

Your mother and brothers, and all of them, send their **very kind** loves, and will welcome your return as heartily as

Your affectionate father,

To ——. (————).

LETTER CXXXII.

To a Veterinary Surgeon.

Suffolk, July 10th. 18—.

Sir,—Please send me (*state the medicine*) for a (*cow or horse, &c.*). He has been bad with the ——, and bleeding seems to have done him no good. Let me know your charge at the same time, and I will send a P.O. for the amount.

Your obedient servant,

To Mr. ——. (————).

LETTER CXXXIII.

The Answer.

Smithfield, 13th July, 18—.

Sir,—I enclose the medicine you wish for, and hope it will do good. Three boluses of the box marked ——, should be given immediately, and a good warm mash will do good, taking care to keep the horse from taking cold. You had better not bleed him any more, until you find how the medicine acts.

The amount you are indebted to me is only ——, which you can either settle by a P O. or leave it towards opening an account.

I am, Sir,

Yours,

To Mr. ——. (————).

LETTER CXXXIV.

To a Clergyman, about rent.

Dorking, October 15th, 18—.

REVEREND AND HONOURED SIR,—In consequence of the failure of the crops during the autumn, I find myself unusually behind-hand, so much so, indeed, that I have been unwillingly compelled to discharge several hands, and cut down all my expenses. I assure you that it is from no desire to deprive you of your just rights that I address you, but I hope that the urgency of the case will be my best apology.

What I have humbly to request is, that you will kindly remit some portion of the tithes due on the —— estate. It has scarcely paid its working expenses during the last two years, and I fear that, at the present rent, I shall be utterly ruined. Knowing well your benevolent disposition, both as a clergyman and a landlord, I hope you will take into consideration my request, and endeavour to make some arrangements by which I may be enabled to retrieve myself from my present diffi-ꞇ ulties.

I remain,

Reverend and honoured Sir,

Your humble and respectful servant,

To the Rev. ——. (————).

LETTER CXXXV.

To the same, on being elected Churchwarden.

October —, 18—.

REVEREND SIR,—I take the liberty of writing a few lines to express my sense of the honour you have conferred upon me in selecting me to act as your senior churchwarden. While I feel that there are many in our district who are more efficient men than myself, I still venture to hope that I shall not be wanting in a sense of the responsibility of my office, and that no conduct of mine will ever disturb that good feeling which should ever exist between the rector and his parish officers.

Again thanking you for the honour thus shown to me,

> I remain,
>> Reverend Sir,
>>> Your obedient and humble servant,

To the Rev ——   (————).

LETTER CXXXVI.

To a relieving Officer, urging a case.

SIR,—The bearer of this note is ——, whom I have known for many years as a hard-working and respectable man. He has never, hitherto, been in any way dependent on the parish, but recent severe illness has incapacitated him from following his usual employment, and has plunged him into a state of distress which drives him to seek relief. I trust, under these circumstances, that you will render him assistance as far as you possibly can, for I feel assured that he will be a claimant on the parish no longer than he can possibly help.

> I am, Sir,
>> Your obedient servant,

To Mr. ——.   (————).

LETTER CXXXVII.

To a Water-Company.

To the Secretary of the Grand Junction Water-Works.

> Kentish Town, 5th July, 18—.

SIR,—I beg to call your attention to the very objectionable state of the water supplied to my house. The supply is irregular, and the quality perfectly unwholesome. I must request the favour of your immediate attention to this serious defect and am,

> Sir,
>> Yours, &c.,

(————).

LETTER CXXXVIII.

To a Theatrical Manager.

Houndsditch, Aug. 8th, 18—

SIR,—Perceiving the announcement that your theatre opens on the —th instant, I write to ask whether you have any vacancy in the scene-painting department. I have had considerable practice, and have painted with some success for the theatres royal ——. Being at present out of engagement, I should gladly join your company, should you be disposed to entertain my proposal.

I remain, Sir,

Your very obedient servant,

To ——, Esq. (———).

LETTER CXXXIX.

In answer to an advertisement for a situation as parish Doctor.

To the Board of Guardians of the ——.

GENTLEMEN,—I beg most respectfully to submit the inclosed diploma and testimonials, as proofs of my qualifications for the office of medical officer now vacant in this parish.

Should you honour me with your confidence, I can only express my determination that no pains shall be spared on my part to satisfy the expectations of those to whose suffrages I may be indebted.

I have the honour to remain,

Gentlemen,

Your most obedient and faithful servant,

(———, M.R.C.S., &c.).

LETTER CXL.

For a situation as parish Clerk.

To the Rector, Churchwardens, and Parishioners of ——.

GENTLEMEN,—Having lived as a ratepayer in this parish —— years, I beg to apply for the situation of parish clerk now vacant. I am considered to have a tolerable voice, and understand sufficient music to be able to lead the psalmody in a parish church.

As a working man, with five children to support, every addition to my means is of importance, and I can assure you that should you select me for the vacant appointment, I shall not only labour earnestly to discharge its duties with propriety, but shall ever remain,

Gentlemen,

Your humble and dutiful servant,

(———).

LETTER CXLI.

For a situation as Organist.*

To the Rector, Churchwardens, and Parishioners of ——.

GENTLEMEN,—In offering myself as a candidate for the vacant situation of organist, I beg to state that I have for —— years held that office in —— church, and, as you will perceive from the inclosed testimonials, with satisfaction to the incumbent and parishioners. Long experience in the various duties of an organist and choir-master leads me to believe that you would not regret your choice, should you honour me with your preference.

On Sunday next, I shall, by permission of the churchwardens, perform on the organ, and shall, during the week, make a private application for your suffrages.

In the hope that my efforts may meet with a result satisfactory to all parties,

I have the honour to remain,

Gentlemen,

Your obedient and faithful servant,

(———).

N.B.—Late organist of ——, master of the choir at —— cathedral, composer of ——.

---

* This is rather a *circular*, than a private letter, but such is the most usual mode of application.

LETTER CXLII.

From a Country Shopkeeper to a Friend in London, desiring him to send him some goods.

Oatlands, March 5th, 18—

DEAR SIR,—That friendship which we contracted in our youth is not yet, I hope, abated, although Providence has placed us many miles distant from each other. I have heard of your success in London, and it is with pleasure I can assure you that I am comfortably settled here. But you know that our returns are slow, and profits small, and therefore, however willing, I am not in circumstances sufficiently good to defray the expenses of a journey to town, in order to purchase goods at the best hand, which will be attended with some loss, because bought at a considerable expense both of time and money. Relying, therefore, on your former friendship, I have presumed to solicit your assistance, to purchase from time to time, such goods as I may happen to want from London, for which an order shall be remitted on delivery. At present I have only sent for a few articles, as you will see by the inclosed. I doubt not of your getting them as good and as cheap as possible; and if there is anything I can do to serve you in this part of the country, you may depend on its being attended to with the utmost fidelity and dispatch.

I am, Sir,

Your sincere friend,

To ——

(————).

LETTER CXLIII.

The Answer.

London, March 7th, 18—.

DEAR SIR,—I duly received yours, and am extremely glad to hear of your being so comfortably settled. There is no small pleasure in hearing that the friends of our youthful days are prospering, and it will give me great delight to think that I have it in my power to be, in any way, of service to my friend. The goods you ordered are sent by the ——Railway, directed to you

They are good, and as cheap as any in London, and I hope you
will be a considerable gainer by their sale. With respect to
your kind proffer of service, I heartily thank you, and shall,
should occasion require, readily avail myself of your kindness.
In the meantime, be sure to command me in everything wherein
I can serve you, as it will give the greatest pleasure to

Your sincere friend,

To ——.   (————).

LETTER CXLIV.

*From a Country Shopkeeper to a dealer in London, complair
ing of the badness of his goods.*

Reading, June 8th, 18—.

SIR,—When I first began to correspond with you, it was my
fixed resolution to act with integrity and honour, expecting the
same conduct in return. I must confess that the goods you
sent me for some time were as good as any I could purchase
from another party, and so far I had no reason to complain.
But the two last parcels sent are so bad, that I dare not offer
them to my customers. Under these circumstances, I am re-
luctantly obliged to tell you, that unless you send me others in
their room, I must either withdraw my correspondence, or shut
my shop. Your immediate answer will oblige,

Yours, &c.

To ——.   (————)

LETTER CXLV.

The Answer to the preceding.

London, June 9th, 18—

SIR,—I received yours, and am extremely sorry to hear the
goods sent you were so bad. I know I had some such in my
warehouse, but was determined to sacrifice them at a low rate,
without ever thinking of their being sent to any of my customers, particularly so regular a correspondent as yourself. By
some mistake my servants have inadvertently sent them, for

which I am extremely sorry; but in order to make you amends, I send by the —— rail those which I had originally intended for you, at my own expense. I hope you will excuse this, and be assured you shall never be served in such a manner for the future.

I am, Sir,
Your humble servant,

To ——,   (—— ——)

LETTER CXLVI.

A Gentleman residing in the country, to a Horse Dealer in London.

Essex, March 29th, 18—.

SIR,—My friend Mr. ——, whom you may remember as having had some dealings with you, has expressed himself so well satisfied with various purchases he has made at your livery stables, that I am induced to rely upon your recommendation in the choice of a horse. I am in want of a good strong hack for ordinary riding, and as I occasionally indulge myself in following the hounds, he should also be equal to that duty : although you must understand that I do not require a professed hunter. The price must be moderate, but I must add, that you must warrant the animal to be free from vice. If you have a horse of this description, you may let him be ridden by a careful groom to my house, on ——, for my inspection. The distance is easy, not exceeding —— miles; and I would call upon you myself were it not for some affairs which detain me at home. If you have nothing likely to suit me, I should be glad if you would write to me to that effect, by an early opportunity, so that I may lose no time in making inquiries elsewhere.

I am, Sir,
Yours obediently,

To Mr. ——.   (—— ——)

LETTER CXLVII.

The Answer.

London, April 3rd, 18—.

SIR,—In obedience to the request contained in your letter of the —— instant, I have dispatched one of my best grooms with a fine young animal, late the property of (   ), who parted with him on account of having occasion to diminish his stud. I have had this horse only a short time in my possession, but on first seeing him was at once struck with the excellence of his points, and the beauty of his proportions. He is — hands high, is rising four years, and was warranted sound, and free from vice. The warranty to that effect I have in my possession, and I should be happy to renew it with you on completing a sale. His price would be £——, and should you be pleased with him, and disposed to make him your own, I would save you the trouble of calling upon me, by riding over to your house at any time to-morrow, or next day, according to your convenience, which you could signify by a letter by the man who brings the horse.

I am, sir,

Your obedient servant,

To ——, Esq.   (———).

LETTER CXLVIII.

From a Circulating Librarian.

Queen's Street, Lincoln's Inn Fields.
March 15th, 18—.

REV. SIR,—I should be much obliged could you spare the first volume of ——, as a member of the library wishes to have a sight of it just now, and the usual time of detention has transpired.

I am, Rev. Sir,

Your most obedient servant,

(———).

To the Rev. T. A. Buckley.

LETTER CXLIX

To a friend in Holy Orders, soliciting his advice.

Buckingham, April 24th, 18—

My dear Sir,—Will you allow me to address a few lines to you on the subject of my desire to study at Oxford for Holy Orders? You have been kind enough to advise me on many points, and also to tell me of many ways by which I might go through the course of study with greater advantages than my present circumstances would permit me to do, *i. e.* if I retain the situation I at present occupy. Amongst others you mentioned the Bible Clerkship at —— College, which you thought, with a little interest, might be obtained in the course of two years, provided that my whole time were given up to reading till the expiration of that period. You will remember that I thought that was then almost an impossibility, from the idea I had that my father would oppose it. You kindly advised me also to make up my own mind and get it settled within three or six months from that time, which was about Christmas last. I have been working very hard since then, both at the office and in the evening at my own home; but as my health has not been very good, I have come down to Buckingham to my father's, where I shall spend a few weeks till I feel a little stronger. I have thus had opportunities of talking over the matter with my father, who was much pleased with the idea of a Bible clerkship at Oriel, and would grant his consent to my resigning at once if there were any probability of my obtaining it. The ——, our Vicar, has promised me what influence he can obtain, and which I have reason to believe is very good; he is cousin to ——, M.P., and his brother is an Examiner, I believe, at —— College.

If, therefore, I am not presuming too much upon your great kindness, may I ask you what would be the best plan to adopt in regard to the attainment of this object; and although I should be sorry either to trespass too much on your valuable time, or give you useless trouble, yet, if I could insure your kindly interest and influence, it would confer a very great favour on me, and one which I should ever appreciate.

As I am likely to remain at home some few weeks at the

least, if a conversation with me would be more serviceable than writing, I would go over to Oxford and call on you; it would be a pleasant trip for me, and would give me great pleasure; but I leave it to your convenience, and can only say that I shall feel very highly gratified by a line or two at your leisure. With many thanks for past favours, and best wishes for your present and future happiness,

> I remain,
> My dear sir,
> Yours very truly,

The Rev. ——.   (———).

LETTER CL.

Proposing an Appointment with the same person.

> Buckingham, April 28th, 18—.

MY DEAR SIR,—I wrote to you at Oxford a few days since (last Tuesday, I think), but as I have not yet received any reply, I conclude you are not staying there at present, but have moved your quarters to town, and, therefore, take the liberty of addressing you at Avenue Terrace.

If you are likely to be at Oxford *this* or *next* week, I intend going over, and would do myself the honour of calling. The favour of a line, therefore, if convenient, per return of post, stating whether I should find you at Christ Church with leisure to grant me an audience of an hour or less, would very greatly oblige,

> My dear Sir,
> Yours very faithfully,

To ——.   (———).

LETTER CLI.

From a Tradesman to a firm.

> Bristol, Jan. 3rd, 18—.

GENTLEMEN,—Enclosed I send you 5*l*., and hope to be able to send the remaining balance of 3*l*. 15*s*. 6*d*. on Saturday next.

I regret being unable to send the whole, but I have been disappointed by not receiving a cheque which was promised a fortnight ago.

I remain,
Gentlemen,
Yours respectfully,

To Messrs. —— and ——.   (————).

LETTER CLII.

In reply to a request for Payment.

London, Aug. 5th, 18—.

GENTLEMEN,—In reply to yours just received, I am sorry to be unable to send you the balance of your account, but will do my utmost to send it the end of this week, or the beginning of next, without fail.

I remain,
Gentlemen,
Your obedient servant,

To Messrs. ——.   (————).

LETTER CLIII.

Another.

Cambridge, June 12th, 18—.

GENTLEMEN,—I regret to be unable to send the amount of your bill in full, but send you 10*l.* by a registered letter. The balance shall be sent on ——, the —th. I fully expected to be able to meet your bill when I wrote to you, and should have done so, but for a severe domestic affliction which has interfered with my paying my usual attention to business. You may, however, rely on my not disappointing you again.

I am,
Gentlemen,
Yours respectfully,

To Messrs. ——.   (————).

LETTER CLIV.

Advice of Money Paid.

Chelmsford, April 4th, 18—.

GENTLEMEN,—We have paid for your application at Messrs.
—— and ——, bankers, Lombard Street, 5*l.* 3*s.*, which, with
2*s.* 4*d.* discount, balances your account to present date.

We are,
Gentlemen,
Your obedient servants,

To Messrs. ——,   (————).

LETTER CLV.

Another.

Leighton, July 15th, 18—.

GENTLEMEN,—If you will be good enough to apply at the
London Joint Stock Bank on ——, they will pay you the sum
of 35*l.* on our account. We have sent this in part payment
of your acceptance due on ——, and with it our acceptance at
two months for the balance. We have been most unwilling to
do this, but we are just now sadly put about by the non-
receipts of some of our largest accounts, and have been obliged
to wait much longer for our money than is by any means
agreeable. But, as they are with parties whom we cannot
press, our circumstances are much crippled.

I shall much esteem your kindness if you will be satisfied
with this arrangement, and remain,

Gentlemen,
Yours faithfully,

To Messrs. ——,   (—— & ——).

LETTER CLVI.

Enclosing Money.

Belfast, March 3rd, 18—.

GENTLEMEN,—Enclosed you have half notes (2nd) for 25*l.*, and postage stamps 14*s.*, to settle our account to ——, viz.:—

Jan 31st.			£	s.	d.
Account rendered	.	. . .	27	10	3
Overcharge on ——		. .	0	14	3
Discount	.	. . .	2	0	0
To Messrs. ——.			25	14	0

LETTER CLVII.

Proposing to open an Account.

Sydney, N. S. Wales, Nov. 30th, 18—.

GENTLEMEN,—Having succeeded to the business formerly carried on by Messrs. ——, we are desirous of entering into a negotiation with your house for the supply of ——. We may mention that business is happily very brisk at present, and that, having materially increased our connection in Melbourne, Adelaide, &c., we flatter ourselves that we could be very instrumental to increasing the sale of ——. We are encouraged to make this application from knowing that you were formerly in the practice of transacting business with Messrs. —— in this way.

We have, in the meantime, forwarded through Messrs. —— a pretty extensive order for your ——, by which you will perceive the nature of the articles most in demand. We would suggest, in the event of your acceding to our application, that a supply of your —— be sent to us, say every six weeks or two months, to the extent of about 150*l.* We mention this sum at present, but hope, when the trial has been made, and we find ourselves in a position regularly to supply our country agents, to have it extended to twice or three times that amount. Mr. ——, who returns to England in the course of a month or two, will give you every satisfaction as to our name and position, but in the meantime we beg to refer you to Messrs. ——, or to Messrs. —— and ——.

We trust the order we have now sent will be executed with all speed, and on presentation of the invoice to Messrs. ——, they will give you a cheque for the amount, as well as advice by what vessel to ship the goods.

We are,
Gentlemen,
Yours obediently,
(—— & ——).

To Messrs. —— & Co.,
—— Street, London.

NOTES, CARDS,* ETC.

An Invitation to Dinner.

Mr. S.'s compliments to Mr. D., and will feel much pleasure in his company to dinner on Thursday next, at six o'clock. An early reply will oblige.

Camden Villas, Thursday, April 19th, 18—.

Reply, accepting the Invitation.

Mr. D. presents his compliments to Mr. S., and accepts with pleasure his invitation for Thursday next.

Eaton Square, Friday, April 20th, 18—.

Declining the Invitation.

Mr. D. presents his compliments to Mr. S., and much regrets that a previous engagement (or continual indisposition, or his unavoidable absence from town) will prevent him from joining Mr. S.'s party on Thursday next.

Eaton Square, Friday, April 20th, 18—.

* Complimentary cards must always have the address, etc., at bottom.

FORMS OF DIRECTING, COMMENCING, AND CONCLUDING LETTERS.

To the Royal Family.

Direct.—To the Queen's (*or* King's) Most Excellent Majesty.

Commence.—Madam (*or* Sire); Most Gracious Sovereign; May it please your Majesty.

Conclude.—I remain, *or*, I have the honour to remain, with the profoundest veneration, *or*, respect, Madam (*or* Sire), your Majesty's most faithful subject and dutiful servant.

Princes of the Blood Royal.

These are only the King's or Queen's sons and daughters, brothers and sisters, uncles and aunts, and are addressed as *Your Royal Highness.*

Princes of the Blood.

Nephews and cousins, who are merely styled, *Your Highness.*

Duke, Princess.

Direct.—To His (*or* Her) Royal Highness the Duke (*or* Princess) of ——.

Commence.—Sir, or Madam.

Conclude.—I remain, with the greatest respect, Sir (*or* I have the honour to remain, Madam), Your Royal Highness's most dutiful and most obedient (*or* most obedient and humble) servant.

o

Nobility and Gentry.

Direct.—To His Grace the Duke (*or* Her Grace the Duchess) of ——.

Commence.—My Lord Duke (*or* Madam).

Conclude.—I have the honour to be, my Lord Duke (*or* Madam), Your Grace's most devoted and obedient (*or* most obedient and humble) servant.

N.B. *Eldest* sons of Dukes are, by courtesy, styled *Marquesses*, but are generally distinguished by their father's *second* title, whether it be that of Marquess or Earl.

Direct.—To the Most Hon. the Marquess (*or* Marchioness) of Lansdowne.

Commence.—My Lord Marquess (*or*, Madam).

Conclude.—I have the honour to be, My Lord Marquess, your Lordship's (*or*, Madam, your Ladyship's) most obedient and most humble servant.

N.B. If the title be taken from *a place*, we prefix *of*, as, " the Marquess *of* Harewood ;" but not so, when it is from a *family name*, as " Earl Stanhope."

Direct.—To the Right Hon. the Earl (*or*, Countess) of Derby.

Commence.—My Lord (Madam).

Conclude.—I have the honour to be, my Lord, your Lordship's (Madam, your Ladyship's) most obedient and humble servant.

N.B. All sons of Dukes and Marquesses, and eldest sons of Earls, have the title of *Lord* and Right Honourable ; and their wives are addressed accordingly.

Direct.—To the Right Hon. Lord Viscount (*or*, Lady Viscountess) ——.

Commence and *Conclude.*—As Earls.

Superscription.—To the Right Hon. Lord (*or*, Lady) ——.

Commence and *Conclude.*—Ditto, ditto.

The *younger* sons of Earls, and *all* the sons of Viscounts and Barons, are styled *Esquire* and *Honourable*, and the daughters and sons' wives, *Honourable*.

Superscription.—To the Honourable ——.

Commence.—Sir.

Conclude.—I have the honour to remain, Sir, your most obedient and humble servant.

Baronets, Knights, and Esquires.

Superscription.—To Sir Peter ——, Bart.

Commence.—Sir (Madam).

Conclude.—I have the honour to be, Sir, your most humble and obedient (*or*, Madam, your Ladyship's most obedient and very humble) servant.

Superscription.—To Sir ——.

Commence and *Conclude* as the last. The title of *Knight* being added only in formal documents; while in a *familiar* address, we generally add the Christian name, as " *Dear* Sir John."

The title of *Esquire* is now given to almost every person of respectability, but in directing to persons of high position and distinction, we generally add &c., &c., &c., writing the word *Esquire* at full length.

The wives of Gentlemen, in cases where several persons of the same family are married, are distinguished by the Christian name of their husbands, *e. g.* Mrs. Frederick Brown, Mrs. Alfred Brown.

The title of *Right Honourable* is also bestowed upon Privy Councillors, upon the Lord Provost of Edinburgh, and the three Lord Mayors, of London, York, and Dublin, during the term of their continuance in office.

The Clergy.

Direct.—To His Grace the Lord Archbishop of ——.

Commence.—My Lord Archbishop.

Conclude.—I remain, My Lord Archbishop, with the highest respect, Your Grace's most devoted and obedient (*or*, humble) servant.

Direct.—To the Right Rev. the Lord Bishop of ——.

Commence.—My Lord Bishop.

Conclude.—I have the honour to be, My Lord, Your Lordship's most obedient humble servant.

———

Direct. — To the Rev. —— ——, D.D. (*or*, to the Rev . ——).

Commence.—Reverend Sir.

Conclude.—I have the honour to be, Reverend Sir, Yours, &c. (*according to the circumstances under which we write, or our acquaintance with the person*).

———

Direct.—To the Very Rev. the Dean of —— (*or*, to the Very Rev. ——, D.D., Dean of ——).

Commence.—Mr. Dean (*or*, Reverend Sir).

Conclude.—I have the honour to be, Mr. Dean (*or*, Reverend Sir, Yours, &c.).

———

Direct.—To the Venerable Archdeacon ——.

Commence.—Reverend Sir.

Conclude.—I remain, Reverend Sir, &c.

NOTE.—When a Bishop or other clergyman possesses the title of *Right Honourable*, or Honourable, it is prefixed to his clerical title. Baronets and Knights, however. have their clerical title placed first.

———

The Officers of Her Majesty's Household

Should be addressed according to their rank, as follows :—

Direct.—To the Right Honourable the Earl of D., Lord High Steward (*or*, Lord High Chamberlain), &c., &c., &c.

Commence.—My Lord Steward (*or*, My Lord Chamberlain).

Letters addressed to any public persons should always have their highest office specified thereon, with three &c. &c. &c. after it.

To the Army and Navy.

In the Army or Navy all Noblemen are styled according to their rank, to which must be added the situation they are employed in—namely:

Direct.—To Lieut.-General Viscount Hardinge, K.C.B., Commander in Chief of Her Majesty's Forces, &c., &c., &c.

Commence.—My Lord (*or*, May it please your Lordship).

Direct.—To Field Marshal the Marquess of Anglesey, K.G., Colonel of the Royal Regiment of Horse Guards (*or*, Master General of the Ordnance), &c., &c., &c.

Commence.—My Lord, Your Lordship.

Direct.—To the Right Hon. Lord Raglan, Commander of Her Majesty's Forces, &c., &c., &c.

Commence.—Sir (*or*, Your Honour).

Direct.—To Colonel the Honourable A. Abercrombie.

Commence.—Sir (*or*, Your Honour).

Direct.—To Major, Captain, or Lieutenant of Her Majesty's 42nd Regiment.

Commence.—Sir.

Direct.—To Sir Charles Napier, K.C.B., Admiral and Commander of the Baltic Fleet, &c., &c., &c.

Commence.—Sir (*or*, Your Honour)

Direct.—To Richard King, Esq., Captain of Her Majesty's Ship Phœbe.

Commence.—Sir, Your Honour.

Direct.—Lieutenant William Norris, R.N., on board Her Majesty's Ship Prince.

Commence.—Sir.

Direct.—Mr. Carter, Midshipman of Her Majesty's Ship Blinker.

Commence.—Sir.

To Ambassadors, Secretaries, Consuls, &c.

Ambassadors have the title of Excellency added to their quality; so have also Plenipotentiaries and Foreign Governors.

Direct.—To His Excellency Lord Howden, Her Britannic

Majesty's Envoy Extraordinary and Plenipotentiary to the
Court of Spain.

Commence.—Sir, Your Excellency.

Direct.—To Signior Fernandez, Secretary from the Republic
of Mexico.

Commence.—Sir.

Direct.—To R. W. Brent, Esq., Consul to Her Britannic
Majesty at Smyrna.

Commence.—Sir.

Direct.—To his Excellency C. M. T., Ambassador to His
Most Christian Majesty.

Commence.—Sir, Your Excellency.

To Judges and Lawyers.

Judges, when Privy Councillors, are styled Right Honourable.

Direct.—To the Right Honourable the Lord High Chancellor
of Great Britain.

Commence.—My Lord, Your Lordship.

Direct.—To the Right Honourable Sir J. L. Knight Bruce,
Vice-Chancellor of England.

Commence.—Sir (*or*, Right Honourable Sir).

Direct.—To the Right Honourable the Master of the Rolls.

Commence.—Sir, Your Honour.

Direct.—To the Right Honourable Lord Campbell, Lord
Chief Justice of the Queen's Bench: [*or* of the Common
Pleas].

Commence.—My Lord, Your Lordship.

Direct.—To the Right Honourable Sir F. Pollock, Lord Chief
Baron of the Exchequer.

Commence.—My Lord, Your Lordship.

Direct.—To Sir E. J. E. Cockburn, Her Majesty's Attorney
(*or* Solicitor) General.

Commence.—Sir.

Observe, that every Barrister has the title of Esquire.

To the Lieutenancy and Magistracy.

Direct.—To the Most Noble the Marquess of Salisbury, Lord Lieutenant of the County of Middlesex, &c., &c., &c.

Commence.—My Lord, Your Lordship.

Direct.—To the Right Honourable the Lord Mayor of the City of London.

Commence.—My Lord, Your Lordship.

Gentlemen acting as Magistrates have the title of Esquire, and are styled Worshipful; so are also Sheriffs and Recorders. The Aldermen and Recorder of London, and the Mayors of all Corporations, excepting London, York, and Dublin, are styled Right Worshipful.

Direct.—To T. E., Esq., High Sheriff of the County of Hants.

Commence.—Sir, Your Worship.

Direct.—To the Worshipful G. H., Esq., one of Her Majesty's Justices of the Peace, for the County of ——.

Commence.—Sir.

To Governors under the Crown.

Direct.—To his Excellency the Earl of St. Germans, Lord Lieutenant of Ireland.

Commence.—My Lord, Your Excellency.

Direct.—To the Right Honourable the Earl of Elgin, Governor-General of Canada, &c., &c., &c.

Commence.—My Lord, Your Lordship.

Direct.—To his Excellency, Charles Fitzgerald, Esq., Governor of Western Australia.

Commence.—Your Excellency.

Direct.—To the Right Honourable Lord L., Governor of Dover Castle, &c., &c., &c.

Commence.—My Lord, Your Lordship.

Direct.—To Major-General Harris, Lieutenant-Governor of Portsmouth.

Commence.—Sir, Your Honour.

To Corporate Bodies.

Direct.—To the Chairman and Directors of the Honourable the East India Company.

Commence.—Gentlemen, Your Honours.

Direct.—To the Honourable the Governor, Deputy-Governor, and Directors of the South Sea Company.

Commence.—Your Honours.

Direct.—To the Honourable the Governor, Deputy-Governor, and Directors of the Bank of England.

Commence.—Your Honours.

Direct.—To the Right Honourable the Lord Mayor, the Worshipful the Alderman, and Common Council, in Common Council.

Commence.—Your Honours.

Direct.—To the Masters and Wardens of the Worshipful Company of Merchant Tailors [Goldsmiths, Stationers], &c.

Commence.—Your Worships.

Concluding Observations.

Some few general remarks on very simple matters—which are nevertheless of much importance in the transactions of every-day life—may be advantageously appended to the speci-mens already laid before the reader.

I. There is great judgment required in using "Sir," or, "Dear Sir," especially in addressing a person of superior worldly position to yourself. Always reflect whether you are on such terms with the person to whom you write as to warrant your using "Dear," or, "My dear," before the more retiring phrase of address.

At the same time, the use of "Dear Sir," even towards a stranger, is considered a graceful manner of addressing an inferior; but, in responding to this, it would be preferable to avoid too much familiarity *at first.* A golden rule in such matters is, that nothing is lost by too much modesty, while nothing gives so much offence as officious familiarity.

"Reverend and dear Sir" is a frequent address from one clergyman to another, with whom he is supposed to have little acquaintance, beyond that of being in the same profession. "Dear Sir" is afterwards adopted, when one or two letters have passed between the parties.

"Dear Sir" is frequently used in transactions between gentlemen and their tradesmen; but such use must be guided by the good sense of both parties. It must also be considered, that the position and character of many tradesmen render them fully on a par with many professional or independent persons.

"Honoured Sir," though somewhat antiquated, is still frequently used, either in addressing a person in very advanced years, a parent, a person to whom we have been under great obligations, or in an appeal from a poor person to a rich and powerful one.

Nearly the same rules apply to letters addressed to persons of the other sex.

II. Never send a *note* to a person who is your superior, unless it be upon a very slight and indifferent matter. In asking a favour of an intimate friend, address him in the first person.

III. Do not take bad writing for freedom of style. Whatever pleasure your friends may derive from reading your letters, you have no right to suppose that they have time for the study of *hieroglyphics*.

IV. And, finally, remember that whatever you write is written evidence either of your good sense or your folly, your industry or carelessness, your self-control or impatience. What you have once put into the letter-box, may cost you lasting regret, or be equally important to your whole future welfare. And, for such grave reasons, *think before you write and think while you are writing.*

APPENDIX.

HAVING thus laid before our readers a few specimens of the art of letter-writing, which we believe will be of service in guiding them, safely and with propriety, through many transactions in life, we propose to give such gentlemen as are not under twenty-one years of age, as well as married ladies (for persons under twenty-one, and married women without the consent of their husbands, cannot make wills), a few directions as to the mode in which they can dispose of their property in legal form, after death. And first of all we would remark that it is *always* advisable, more especially if it is wished to tie up property in any particular manner, or, as it is technically called, "to settle it," to consult some respectable attorney on the subject; it will be the cheaper course in the end: but if our readers determine to dispose of their property themselves, then let the following directions be carefully attended to.

Write down clearly and simply what you wish to do with your property, somewhat in the same way as you would express your wishes on the subject to a friend, and in some such way as this:—"I, X. Z., of ——, give my furniture and household effects to A., my money in the funds to B., a legacy of £10 to C.," and so on, concluding in some such words as these: "And I give all the rest of my property to D., for his own use and benefit, and appoint him my executor." Care must be taken that there are no alterations or interlineations in the will; in fact, if any errors should be made in writing it out, it will be better to write a fresh copy. Sign the will under the last line thereof,

in the presence of two witnesses, who must sign their names as
witnesses, in your presence, and in each other's presence; that
is, before any one leaves the room; and it is to be observed,
that the witnesses must not be persons who take any benefit
under the will, or the bequest or legacy to such witnesses would
be void.

And now, having given directions how to make a will, let us
tell you how to revoke it; the will may be revoked by your exe-
cuting a new one, or destroying the old, and it will be well to
bear in mind that a will is revoked by the marriage of the
testator.

A few simple forms of wills are here added, which may be
useful to our readers, as helping them to carry out their inten-
tions towards those who are to come after them.

It is particularly recommended that the attestation clause
should always be written just above the place where the witnesses sign their names, as it will save a little expense in proving the will.

———

*Form of a Will in which property is left to one or more
persons absolutely.*

This is the last Will and Testament of me —— of ——.
I direct that all my just debts, funeral and testamentary expenses be paid and satisfied by my Execut
hereinafter named, as soon as conveniently may be after
my decease. I give and bequeath to —— all my household furniture, linen, wearing apparel, books, plate, pictures, china, horses, carts, and carriages, and also, all
and every sum and sums of money which may be found
in my house, or be about my person, or due to me at
the time of my decease, and also all my stocks, funds, and
securities for money, book-debts, money on bonds, bills,
notes, or other securities, and all and every other item
of my estate, and effects whatsoever and wheresoever, both
real and personal, whether in possession or reversion, remainder, or expectancy, to and for —— own use and benefit
absolutely. And I nominate, constitute, and appoint ——
to be Execut—— of this my Will, and hereby revoking all

other Wills and Testaments by me at any time heretofore
made, I declare this to be my last Will and Testament.
In witness whereof I the said —— have to this my last
Will and Testament, set my hand the —— day of ——, in
the year of our Lord, one thousand eight hundred and ——.

Signed by the Testat

> *(Signature of Testator*
> *or Testatrix .* }   _____

and acknowledged by h——
to be h— last Will and
Testament, in the presence
of us present at the same
time, and subscribed by us
in the presence of the said
Testat— and of each other.

Attesting Witnesses.

_____

_____

_____

_____

---

*Will in which property is devised to executors in trust, to be
sold, and to pay proceeds to any number of persons therein
mentioned.*

This is the last Will and Testament of me —— of ——

I direct that all my just debts, funeral and testamentary expenses be duly paid and satisfied, by my Executors
hereinafter named, as soon as conveniently may be after
my decease. I give, devise, and bequeath all my household furniture, linen, wearing apparel, books, plate, china,
pictures, horses, carts, and carriages. And also, all and
every sum and sums of money, which may be found in
my house, or be about my person, or due to me, at the
time of my decease. And also, all my stocks, funds, and
securities for money, money due on bonds, bills, notes or
other securities, and all and every other my estate and effects,
whatsoever, and wheresoever, whether in possession or reversion, remainder or expectancy, unto —— and the survivor of them, and the executors and administrators of such
survivor or survivors upon trust, as soon as conveniently

may be after my decease, to collect, get in, and receive such parts thereof as shall consist of money or securities for money, and to sell, dispose of, and convert into money all other parts of my real and personal estate, either by public auction, or private contract, as to my said Executors seems right. And upon further trust when, and so soon as the whole of my real and personal estate shall have been converted into money, and received, upon trust to pay —— equal —— part or share thereof, unto —— of —— for —— own use and benefit. And to pay —— other equal —— part or share thereof, unto —— of —— for —— own use and benefit, and to pay one other equal —— part or share thereof unto —— of —— for —— own use and benefit, and to pay over the remaining equal —— part or share thereof unto —— of —— for —— own use and benefit. And I direct that the receipts of my said Executors for the purchase-money of my real or personal estate shall be good and sufficient discharges to the purchasers thereof, and that such purchasers shall not be obliged to see to the application thereof. And I do hereby nominate, constitute, and appoint —— Executors of this my Will. And I do hereby declare that my said Executors and the survivor of them, and the Executors and Administrators of such survivor shall and may at all times out of the first monies that may come to their or either of their hands, reimburse and indemnify themselves and himself respectively, for all such costs, damages, charges, and expenses as they, or either of them, may be put to or sustain in and about the execution of the trusts of this my Will, and that neither of them shall be answerable for any loss which may happen to the said trust premises, unless the same shall happen by or through his or their wilful neglect, or default, nor for any loss which may happen from depositing any of the trust monies in the hands, keeping, or custody of any public Banker, nor the one for the other of them, neither shall either of them be answerable for more monies than shall actually come into his hands by virtue of this my Will. And hereby revoking and making void all former or other Wills by me at any other time heretofore made, I do declare this to be my last Will and Testament

In Witness whereof I the said —— have to this my last
Will and Testament set my hand the —— day of
—— in the year of our Lord one thousand eight hundred
and ——.

Signed by the Testat

Signature of Testator}
or Testatrix . .}   _____

and acknowledged by h—
to be h— last Will and
Testament in the presence
of us present at the same
time, and subscribed by us
in the presence of the said
Testat— and of each other.

Attesting Witnesses.

_____

_____

_____

———

Will. Property left to Wife absolutely.

This is the last Will and Testament of me —— made this ——
day of —— one thousand eight hundred and —— as follows :—I give devise and bequeath all my messuages, lands,
tenements, and hereditaments, and all my household furniture, ready money, securities for money, money secured by
Life Assurance, goods and chattels, and all other parts of my
real and personal estate, and effects whatsoever, and wheresoever, unto my dear Wife —— her heirs, executors, administrators, and assigns, to and for her and their own abso-
lute use and benefit, according to the nature and quality
thereof respectively, subject only to the payment of my
just debts, funeral, and testamentary expenses, and the
charges of proving and registering this my Will. And I
appoint my said Wife Executrix of this my Will, and
hereby revoke all other Wills. In Witness whereof, I
have hereunto set my hand and seal the day and year above
written.

Signed by the Testator

Signature of Testator _____

Signed, sealed, published
and acknowledged by the
said
as and for his last Will
and Testament, in the
presence of us, who in his
presence, and at his re-
quest, and in the presence
of each other, have sub-
scribed our names as wit-
nesses.

Attesting Witnesses.

_____

_____

_____

---

*Will. Property left to Wife, for life or widowhood, and after
her death to Children, with provision for maintenance
during minority, &c. Legacies to Executors.*

This is the last Will and Testament of me ——, of No. —,
—— Street, in the parish of ——, in the town of ——,
merchant. I give, devise, and bequeath, unto my executors hereinafter-named, all my estate and effects, real and
personal, that I may die possessed of or entitled to, in possession or expectancy, upon trust, to be, as soon as conveniently can be after my decease, sold and converted into
money, and the proceeds invested in one or other of the
public funds, and the dividends arising therefrom to be
paid, yearly and every year, unto my dear wife Susan B.,
during the term of her natural life, should she so long continue my widow; the first yearly payment thereof to commence and be payable at the expiration of the first year
after my decease; and after the decease or second marriage
of my said wife, whichever event shall first happen, I
direct my said executors to divide the whole of the said
principal trust fund equally among all my children by my
said wife, the share of each child to be paid on his or her
respectively attaining the age of twenty-one years; and I
direct that the dividends arising therefrom shall be applied,

at the discretion of my executors, towards the maintenance and education of my said children, until they shall severally and respectively attain the said age. And in case any or either of my said children shall happen to die under twenty-one, then I give and bequeath the share or shares of him, her, or them, so dying, unto the survivors or survivor of them.

And I nominate and appoint Mr. ——, of ——, and Mr. ——, of ——, and the survivor of them, and the executors or administrators of such survivor, to be executors or executor of this my Will; and in consideration of the trouble thus imposed on them, I do hereby give and bequeath unto each of my said executors the legacy or sum of one hundred pounds, free of legacy duty and all other deductions. And hereby revoking all former or other Wills by me at any time made, I the said —— do this, which I declare to be my last Will and Testament, as witness my hand this —— day of ——, 18—.

Signed by the Testator

Signature of Testator _____

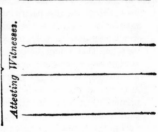

Signed by the said Testator and acknowledged by him to be his last Will and Testament in the presence of us present at the same time, and subscribed by us in the presence of the said Testator, and of each other.

Attesting Witnesses.

——

A common Bond.

Know all Men by these presents, that I —— of —— am held and firmly bound to —— of —— in the sum of —— of good and lawful money of Great Britain, to be paid to the said —— or his certain Attorney, Executors, Administrators, or Assigns, for which payment to be well and faithfully made I bind myself, my Heirs, Executors and Administrators, firmly by these presents. Sealed, with my Seal. Dated this —— day of —— in the year of our Lord one thousand eight hundred and fifty ——.

. Under such a Bond as this the whole sum mentioned might be recovered.

Form of Bond, with a Condition.

Know all Men by these Presents, that I —— of —— am held and firmly bound to —— in the penal sum of £—— of good and lawful money of Great Britain, to be paid to the said —— or his certain Attorney, Executors, Administrators or Assigns, for which payment to be well and faithfully made I bind my Heirs, Executors, or Administrators firmly by these presents. Sealed with my Seal. Dated this —— day of —— in the year of our Lord one thousand eight hundred and fifty ——.

The Condition of the above-written bond or obligation is such, that if the above bounden —— his Heirs, Executors, or Administrators shall and do well and truly pay and cause to be paid unto the above named —— his Executors, Administrators, or Assigns, the full sum of —— of lawful money of Great Britain, then this obligation to be void, or else to be and remain in full force and virtue.

(*Here follow the Signatures.*)

Signed sealed and delivered ⎫
in the presence of . . . ⎭

Form of Transfer of a Share in a Public Company or Undertaking.

I —— of ——.

In consideration of the sum of —— paid to —— by —— Do hereby bargain, sell, assign and transfer to the said —— Share —— Numbered —— of and in the undertaking called the ——

P

To hold unto the said —— executors, administrators, and assigns, subject to the several conditions on which —— held the same immediately before the execution hereof. And —— the said —— do —— hereby agree to accept and take the said —— Share —— subject to the conditions aforesaid :

As witness our hands and seals this —— day of —— in the year of our Lord one thousand eight hundred and ——.

Signed, Sealed, and Delivered }
by the above-named —— in }
the presence of . . . . . }

Witness's name, address, }
and profession . . . }

Signed, Sealed, and Delivered }
by the above-named —— in }
the presence of . . . . . }

Witness's name, address, }
and profession . . . }

Signed, Sealed, and Delivered }
by the above-named —— in }
the presence of . . . . . }

Witness's name, address, }
and profession . . . }

———

Form of Proxy to enable any Partner or Shareholder in any Public Company, or Undertaking, to act or vote for another Partner or Shareholder.

I —— of —— one of the Proprietors of —— of and in the —— do hereby nominate constitute and appoint —— of —— to be my Proxy, in my name, and in my absence to vote and give my assent to, or dissent from any business, matter or thing relating to the said Undertaking, which shall be mentioned or proposed at —— of the said —— to be holden at —— on —— the —— day of —— one thousand eight hundred and —— or at any adjournment of the said Meeting, in such manner as the said —— shall think proper according to his opinion and judgment for the benefit of the said undertaking or anything relating thereto.

In witness whereof I have hereunto set my hand the —— day of —— in the year of our Lord one thousand eight hundred and ——.

Note.—This Proxy cannot be used at any other Meeting than the one specially above-named, or an adjournment of the same Meeting. It cannot be stamped after being signed; and any person voting upon an unstamped Proxy, or voting at two or more distinct Meetings upon the same Proxy, or signing an unstamped Proxy, is liable to a penalty of £50 —7 Vict., cap. 21.

FORMS OF PETITIONS, ETC.

The following forms, &c., &c., may also be useful to some of our readers.*

A Petition for a place in the Inland Revenue Office.

To the Right Honourable the First Lord of the Treasury.

The humble petition of ——, of

Showeth,

That your Lordship's petitioner, being anxious to procure an appointment under Government, is induced to prefer the Inland Revenue Service, from an opinion that, from his education, habits, and manners, he is better calculated to discharge the duties of that department than any other.

Your Lordship's petitioner therefore humbly ventures to solicit an appointment as   in the above-mentioned service; and he is the more induced to hope for success in his humble petition thus presented to the notice of your Lordship, from the circumstance that his character will bear the test of inquiry; and, if necessary, your Lordship's petitioner can produce a variety of the most respectable testimonials as to the general propriety of his conduct.

And your Lordship's petitioner, as in duty bound, will ever pray, &c.

* It is, however, generally advisable to have information as to the *precise form* to be adopted, as the wording of a petition must be considerably varied, according to the nature of the subject, the person addressed, &c.

Memorial from a Widow, to solicit for her Son a situation in
   one of the Government or Public Establishments.

To the Honourable the Chairman and Commissioners of
   the Board of Inland Revenue.

The Memorial of Maria Stevens, widow of the late
   Thomas Stevens, of ——, in the county of ——,

Humbly and respectfully showeth,

That your Memorialist's late husband was for —— years in
the employ of the Inland Revenue Department, as a ——, the
duties of which, as your Memorialist has always understood,
he fulfilled with credit to himself and to the satisfaction of his
superior officers.

That by his death, after a protracted illness of —— duration,
your Memorialist is left a widow, with —— children, unpro-
vided for, and dependent on her exertions for support: and of
which number, the eldest is now in the (sixteenth) year of his
age; and, as your Memorialist has been informed, is in all
respects eligible to fulfil the duties of some situation in the
Inland Revenue Department.

Under these circumstances, your Memorialist is induced
humbly and respectfully to solicit from your Honourable
Board any appointment which may be vacant, and for which,
in the opinion of your Honourable Board, he may be competent.

And your Memorialist will ever pray.

Recommended by—

————

Memorials to the East India Company should be addressed :—
   To the Chairman and Directors of the Honourable the East
   India Company.
To the West India (or other) Dock Company—to be addressed :
   —To the Chairman and Directors of the (West India) Dock
   Company, London.
Railway Boards are addressed :—To the Chairman and Direc-
   tors of the (North Western) Railway Company.

— — —

The preceding Memorial will form a pretty good model for a
petition to solicit for a son an admission into the Blue Coat

School, Hertford School, or other public school of a similar kind, by merely varying the wording of the memorial, so as to state the particulars of the case in a brief and truthful manner.

For information as to exhibitions and other such matters belonging to public schools, companies, &c., the reader is referred to the *Liber Scholasticus.*

VARIOUS FORMS OF RECEIPTS, BILLS, ETC.

⁎ By the New Law of Receipts a Penny Stamp is to be used for any sum amounting to £2 or upwards.

A Receipt for Money.

London, August 4th, 18—.

Received from Mr. Eaton, five pounds, seven shillings, and eight-pence, amount of account delivered.

£5   7s.   8d.   CHARLES FOX.

A Receipt in full of all Demands.

Canterbury, April, 18—.

Received of —— Esq., the sum of —— pounds —— shillings and —— pence being in full of all demands to the present time.

s.   d.   JONES, LLOYD AND CO.

A Receipt for Rent.

London, October 7th, 18—.

Received of Mr. William Jackson, ten pounds, for one quarter's rent of the house, No. 6, White Street, Bermondsey, due Michaelmas day last.

£10   0s.   0d.   JOHN HARTLEY.

A Bill of Exchange.

£50   6s.   0d.   London, November 12th, 18—.
                Two months after date pay to us or our order
                the sum of fifty pounds six shillings, for value
                received.

                                      ALLAN AND GIBBS.

To Mr. Francis Peter,
    23, Fitzroy Square, London.

————

A Banker's Draft.

£75   6s.   London, January 19th, 18—.
At ten days' sight, pay to Messrs. —— and Jones, or order,
the sum of seventy-five pounds six shillings, for value received,
and place the same to my account.
                I am, Sir,
                      Your obedient servant,
To Messrs. —— and ——.   (————).

Note.—To render the above bills current, or negotiable, they must be
accepted by the person on whom drawn and endorsed by the drawer, as
well as by all persons through whose hands they may pass. They may
be of any date, as agreed on by the parties.

————

A Promissory Note.

£35.   London, June 4th, 18—.
Two months after date, I promise to pay to Mr. William
Long, or his order, the sum of thirty-five pounds, for value re-
ceived.

                                      (————).

Payable at Messrs. —— and ——
    Bankers, Pall Mall.

Note.—This bill, to render it negotiable, must be endorsed by the
party to whom the note is made payable and the persons whose hands it
may pass through, in the same manner as directed for bills of exchange.

Bills must not be dated before the day on which they are drawn, or a
penalty of £100 will be incurred.

SIXPENNY MINIATURE LIBRARY.

Cloth, gilt edges.   (Postage 1d.)

The Language of Flowers.
Etiquette for Gentlemen.
Etiquette for Ladies.
Etiquette of Courtship and Matrimony.
The Ball-Room Manual.
Carving.
Toasts and Sentiments.
How to Dress Well.

SHILLING SONG BOOKS

EDITED AND COMPILED BY J. E. CARPENTER.

Fcap. 24mo, boards, with fancy covers.   (Postage 2d.)

The Modern Song Book.
The Popular Song Book.
New Universal Song Book.
The Comic Song Book.
The Humorous Song Book.
The New British Song Book.
Entertainer's Song Book.
The New Standard Song Book.
The Comic Vocalist.
The New Scotch Song Book.
The New Irish Song Book.
The Moral Song Book.
The Religious Song Book.

SIXPENNY SONG BOOKS

EDITED BY J. E. CARPENTER.

Each 144 pp., fcap. 24mo, fancy covers.   (Postage 1d.)

The Fireside Song Book.
The Home Songster.
The British Song Book.
Songs for All Ages.
The Select Songster.
The Convivial Songster.
Merry Songs for Merry Meetings.
Funny Man's Song Book.
Fashionable Song Book.
The Drawing-Room Song Book.
The Laughable Song Book.
The Sensation Songster.
Everybody's Song Book.
The Sociable Song Book.
The Family Song Book.
The Amusing Songster.
The Social Songster.
Songs for All Seasons.
The Droll Ditty Song Book.
The Whimsical Songster.
The Highland Songster.
The Blue Bell Songster.
The Shamrock Songster.
The Mavourneen Songster.
The Sacred Songster.
The Devout Songster.
Songs for the Righteous.
Songs of Grace.

Everybody's Song Book. Words and Music. By Rev. GUISE TUCKER, M.A., and C. H. PURDAY.   2s.

Hearty Staves of Heart Music. By Rev. J. E. CLARKE.   4d.

USEFUL LIBRARY

In fcap. 8vo, boards, 1s. each.

Home Book of Household Economy. ANNE BOWMAN.

Common Things of Every- day Life. ANNE BOWMAN.

Mrs. Rundell's Cookery.

Tricks of Trade in the Adulteration of Food and Physic.

Common Objects of the Microscope. By Rev. J. G. WOOD, with 400 Illustrations by TUFFEN WEST.

Hints for the Table. JOHN TIMBS. [FREEDLEY]

How to Make Money.

Infant Nursing. Mrs. PEDLEY. [Mrs. PEDLEY.]

Practical Housekeeping.

Ready-made Speeches.

Gazetteer of Great Britain and Ireland. 1s. 6d.

The Dinner Question. TABITHA TICKLETOOTH.

How to Dress on £15 a Year as a Lady. By a Lady.

How to Economise like a Lady. By Author of "How to Dress on £15 a Year."

Breakfast, Luncheon, and Tea. MARION HARLAND.

How we Managed without Servants. By a Lady who can Help. [quette.

Shilling Manual of Eti-

The Pleasures of House- building: A Story of Struggle and Adventure. J. FORD MACKENZIE.

The Electric Light, with 35 Illusts. T. C. HEPWORTH.

Practical Penmanship; or, How to Become a Good Writer. W. D. PRIOR.

In fcap. 8vo, cloth, 1s. each.

Ladies' and Gentlemen's Letter Writer.

*Law of Landlord and Tenant. W. A. HOLDSWORTH.

*Law of Wills, Executors, and Administrators. With the Acts of 1881. Ditto.

Commercial Letter Writer

*Education Act. Ditto.

*New Law of Master and Servant. Ditto.

*Ballot Act. Ditto.

*Law of Bills, Cheques and IOU's. W. A. HOLDSWORTH.

Guide to London. Revised

*Friendly Societies' Act. W. A. HOLDSWORTH.

A Practical Guide to Eco- nomical Furnishing.

Soyer's Shilling Cookery for the People.

*Weights and Measures Acts. W. A. HOLDSWORTH.

* " POPULAR LAW BOOKS," Fcap. 8vo, cloth, 1s. each.

Fcap. 8vo, cloth, 2s. each.

Landmarks of the His- tory of England. Rev. JAMES WHITE.

Landmarks of the His- tory of Greece. Ditto.

Edwards' History of France. New and Revised Edition.

Goldsmith's History of England.